The face of Dhamma

by
Michael Kewley
Dhammachariya Paññadipa

All rights reserved.

No part of this publication may be reproduced, stored in a retrieval system or transmitted, in any form or by any means, electronic, mechanical, photocopying, recording or otherwise, without prior permission of the publishers.

This book is sold subject to the condition that it shall not by way of trade or otherwise, be lent, re-sold, hired out or otherwise circulated without the publishers prior consent in any form of binding cover other than that in which it is published and without similar condition including this condition being imposed on the subsequent purchaser.

Copyright © Michael Kewley 2019

ISBN: 978-1-899417-22-3

Published by:
Panna Dipa Books.

Format and cover photograph:
Tiger Hill © Isabelle Kewley 2019

e-mail:
dhammateacher@hotmail.com

Dedication

To all the disciples of Dhamma
who make their practice in the world day by day.
May you all be well and happy.

The face of Dhamma

We teach what we have learned.
We share what we have understood.
May all beings be happy.

Foreword.

At one time there was a monk who lived a solitary life in the middle of a forest.
He stayed alone and sat in meditation both day and night.
However, this monk was so full of love and wisdom that every morning he would walk to the forest clearing where he had created a large semi circle of stones, and taking the teachers place, share his Dhamma understanding with them.

For five years I lived something of a reclusive life with my wife and three cats in a large forest in the department of Les Landes in France.
It was an idyllic time for me, surrounded by the green of the trees and the sounds of nature, where the wild deer would tentatively come right up to the house and eat the grass as I would sit and meditate in the early morning. The wild pigs would stay further away at the far end of our parcel of land, but they were always equally welcome.
However, it was an isolated life, and apart from travelling to teach and share Dhamma, we stayed quite alone in our little family and wildlife paradise.
Therefore it was an interesting moment when my sons informed me about Facebook, and how I should use it to put Dhamma into the world.
It seemed to be a wonderful opportunity and so I began. It was my circle of stones in the forest clearing.
Slowly, slowly I began writing and offering short Dhamma talks to share my heart and then being pleased to accept interested people as Facebook friends.
Now some years later I have collected many of these talks and gathered them together here. They are in a completely random order and so they can be read simply by opening the book at any

page, or more methodically, beginning with the first talk and reading through to the end.

It is really up to you.

Read one or two a day, and reflect upon the purity of the message. As with every book I have written the only reason to produce such a work is to support you in your daily practice, and to remind you to stay on the Path of Dhamma.

We are not monks or nuns living protected lives in a monastery or Vihara, but rather ordinary people, working and interacting with the world at large.

Because of this I feel it is useful to have the Dhamma presented in a way that is relevant to our daily life. After all, that is exactly what the Buddha did two thousand five hundred years ago in northern India.

The Dhamma here is the same, only the language is different.

May you be well and happy.

Introduction

Our practice in the world

I can honestly say that my greatest passion and joy is to share the teachings of Pure Dhamma with disciples and students who have the intention to train in the Way of Love and Awareness.

I endeavour always to present these beautiful teachings which are not tainted by religion, dogma or personal views and opinions, and encourage all my disciples and students to 'look only within', for the truth.

I trained with a Master for more than twenty years who sent me into the world to offer these teachings so that others might benefit as I have benefited.

Now, as I grow older, it is my earnest Dhammic desire to serve as many beings as possible with the beauty and directness of this Dhamma whether in person or through the simple words presented here.

These daily reminders are offered to support our practice and developing understanding as we live our day to day ordinary life.

The truth is apparent in every moment and in every situation, and all we have to do is turn our face to the goal of freedom, not from our external environment, but from the trap of the mind, filled as it is with our myriad views and opinions as to how everyone and everything should be.

Dhamma understanding is not about a superficial agreement with a tradition or the teacher, it is about the personal and intuitive realisation that it is the thoughts we empower that make the world we experience. When these thoughts are established in fear, our life becomes fearful. When they are established in love, our life becomes loving.

The equations in Dhamma are always very simple and so the true disciple lives their life with Love and Awareness and serves the world to ease the suffering of themselves and all beings. This is the Way of Dhamma.

>   May all beings be happy.

>   Michael Kewley
>   Dhammachariya Paññadipa

>   Mirepoix
>   France
>   March 2019

Living Dhamma.

The thing that you need to be clear about is 'what is it that I want?' If you can't find clarity in that, you need to ask, 'what is it that I don't want?'

These are huge questions because ultimately, the ending of unhappiness and frustration in life comes from the relinquishing of a self identity. Just that very notion demands a deep investigation. In the end it is only ever this narrow and limited self identity who struggles with life. This apparent being who desires and fears, who chooses one life above another, who loves and hates. When there is no attachment or belief in this self identity there is only the harmonious flow and the resultant beingness with life.

No fight, no struggle, no pain.

Chasing happiness by continually following thoughts and endless desires will always in the end, be disappointing.

It's the trick of the mind to think, once I have all the things I can imagine as life fulfilling I'll be happy forever. The cause of our unhappiness is the mind's relationship to life. It is the beginning and ending of our suffering. This is the place to start. Even if you complain about your life, you are still blessed. You have food, clothes, money, freedom, all those things, but it's still not enough. Reflect, when will it ever be enough? If you have £1,000,000 you want £2,000,000.

If you want a worldly life that's fine of course, and there are many things you can enjoy, but whether your path is spiritual or mundane, you still have to make your own effort. There are no quick fixes for anything that has value.

May you and all beings be happy.

The unavoidable spiritual reality.

To understand life you must understand the mind.
To understand the mind you must understand kamma.
To understand kamma you must practice profound Love and Awareness meditation.
Without understanding the kammic forces in your life, whatever you do you are always dancing around the edges of liberation.
Kamma is not a secret, it is a truth that everyone has to live with. What we meet in every moment of our life is the consequence of that which we have empowered in the past.
However, because kamma is subtle, we very often don't understand its reality and so cultivate fantastic ideas about it. We think that if a tin of paint falls on our head as we walk under a ladder or we are infected with a terrible disease, that is our kamma. We think that if we are successful with a job application, or fall in love with a beautiful person, that is our kamma.
However, whatever these things are and however we may want to speak about them, they are not kamma.
To understand the truth of kamma, we must investigate for ourselves its origins and what kamma really means in our life.

May all beings be happy.

Compromise.

Dhamma understanding is very subtle and so can often sound contradictory, but there is a difference between compromise, and generously sharing the best part of yourself with others.
If you don't mind what you do there is no compromise. You will enter into the moment and bring something of worth.
If you do mind you must say no and honour your ideals and principles.
Compromise usually means giving up something you want for the apparent happiness of someone else, but this is always a big trap and may develop into a businessman's relationship to the situation. Exchanging one thing for another.
Integrity means to stay true to those things that have value for you, if not there will often be a feeling of hostility or resentment.
When the heart is open, we can flow with the ever changing conditions of life and not mind where they take us, but we always need to guard our own centre. However we look at it, your life is about you and when you are comfortable with you, you will share that happiness. Your life will be clear and you will understand the simplicity of integrity.
Whenever you are doing something that you don't want to do you need to ask yourself this simple question; 'If I don't want to do this, why am I doing it?'
The head may offer a thousand reasons, but the truth is simple; we find ourselves living a life or doing things that we don't want to do because we are afraid of the perceived opinion of others, of losing something or being regarded as an outcast.
However, it is better to be alone than live a life of delusion and compromise.
I can never tell you what you should or should not do, but the Dhamma advice is to listen to your heart and not be directed by fear. In other words, do not compromise those things that are

important for you.
In the end, each step on the Dhamma Path is a step of integrity, and this is what has value.

May you and all beings be happy.

Judgement.

One time on retreat in India a young man came to me and said, "Whenever I close my eyes to meditate, I hear Beatles songs in my head, what shall I do?"
My reply was simple and immediate, "Let it be."
The song is not the problem, it's singing along that brings the difficulties.

In our Vipassana training, awareness means to see the movements of mind without commenting upon them or judging what is observed.
The moment we interact with what the mind presents we spin the kammic wheel one more time and so are never completely free.
This is how life is for most people, to believe what the mind tells them and so immediately act upon it, whether physically in the material world or emotionally in the world of mental fantasies.
Judgement of others is natural in beings and has its roots in fear.
However it makes no sense for the teacher to simply say, 'stop judging others,' as judgement is a habitual movement of mind cultivated over many, many years in many situations and comfortably supported by the society we are part of. Better to say, 'be peaceful with what the mind presents, make the space for this old story to show itself but don't act on it. Don't empower it with either indulgence or repression but simply let it be.'
In this way the habit will naturally become weaker and you will allow the habit of judging yourself and others to quietly dissolve. However, you will observe. You will see now with eyes no longer distorted by prejudice.
This is important to understand. You will observe the way of the world, and the behaviour of beings living in the world. You will not be blind to cruelty or unkindness, or the lack of honesty or integrity in fellow beings, you will just not judge it from your

own position of fear. Do you understand?

You will live from Love and an open heart and not be deluded by what you meet from the world, whether internally or externally. You will respond to life as you meet it with kindness and a smile and not give away your energy to an old habit that brings no benefit.

Judgement brings no peace in life and because beings will always meet the consequence of the mind states they empower there is never a need for anyone to impose their own personal views, opinions and judgements on the unfolding universe we are a part of.

Therefore the Dhamma teaching is always the same; take care of yourself and live with love and be aware.

May all beings be happy.

'You' is only a moment.

The greatest gift we can bring to ourselves and ultimately the whole universe, is the impartial and true understanding of mind.

Without this supremely important investigation and its consequent understanding, we will empower delusion after delusion and accept whatever manifests in our internal world as truth, rather than the simple reality of moments of mind arising and passing away.

Everything in your life is about your relationship to this mind that you call yours. It is the world you inhabit and then project outward into the material world.

Without understanding this relationship you will always arrive in the place of discontent and unhappiness as the dreams you chase as realities always unravel before your very eyes.

If you cannot control this mind, how will you control the minds of others?

If you cannot lovingly accept the thoughts of yourself, how will you lovingly accept the thoughts of others?

However you can argue, life is only about movements of mind, of personal, social, gender or religious ideas, indoctrinated into you. None of them are you, none of them are yours and none of them are what you are.

They are only clouds in a clear blue sky, and all only ever have the power that you give them.

Let go, let go, let go, and stop being a prisoner to this dream state.

The less of 'you' there is the happier life will be - for all beings.

The less of 'you' there is, the more love the world will receive.

'You' in any moment is only a thought.

May all beings be happy.

The worldly life and the Dhamma life.

There are two lives; the worldly life and the Dhamma life.
The worldly life begins at birth where we receive our social, cultural and gender conditioning. We are told how to behave to be accepted by our peers, what to believe to be accepted as part of our particular religious grouping and what to expect from life as part of our social status and position in society.
Based upon our own kammic dispositions we either accept, reject or compromise these various conditionings to take our place in the world. This is the birth that everybody takes.
Birth into a true Dhamma life is rare and at least at the beginning, beset with difficulties.
A small voice inside continually questions what is presented as fact and rebels against an unquestioning acceptance of authority.
From this position we seek answers to simple yet disturbing questions; why is life like this, why must I conform to the norm and how can I be free?
Our Dhamma investigation takes us always to one place, to the very cause of all our difficulties - the belief in a true and permanent self!
If we are brave enough we will begin to lovingly and patiently dismantle this insidious identification with a fantasy, slowly letting go, letting go, letting go of the cause of our difficulties.
And it is this very process that differentiates the worldly life from the Dhamma life.
It is not about destroying 'self', but only being free from the delusion that it is real and must always be satisfied by the world and every being in it!
The highest teaching and the greatest freedom is to live in the world yet not be part of the world. To understand that all our happiness and unhappiness comes only from ourselves and that we are actually helpless in the spiritual or emotional lives of

others. Once we fully realise this we can be at peace, sharing what we know without expectation and offering our now unconditional Love to all beings.

May all beings be happy.

The beautiful Way of Dhamma.

Because the world is filled with unenlightened beings, the potential for cruel and selfish actions exists without limitations. Our homes are bombarded by images and sounds that can fill us with horror, and because of our own fear, it is easy to become confused and entrapped by the madness of the world, always looking for our own position to take. Who is right? Who is wrong? What should be done?

The Way of Dhamma is to stay in balance and allow the world to be as it is, responding as we need to, but letting go of all judgement and recrimination and transcending the limitations of fear. Beings are the way they are, that's their choice, but you are the way you are, and that's your choice! So how are you choosing to be today?

The moment we defend, support or rationalise violent action, whether through mind, body or speech, we have joined the ranks of the unenlightened and forgotten our heart.

All the great Masters, past and present speak of Love as the answer to all the difficulties of the world, but it is for true disciples of Dhamma to hear these words, not only with their ears, but with their heart and their whole being, and then apply them to their life. This is how we give ourselves to Dhamma.

May all beings be happy

The power of Love.

The world is filled with unawakened beings. That's why it is the way that it is. That's why you see what you see. It's why you see the violence and cruelty, segregation and gender inequality and it's why you see and feel the fear and nonsense that pervades everything. That constant, endless distraction away from simply being still and meeting the simplicity of the mind.
Reflect, where can you go now to find a silent place?
They are really rare.
Music, aeroplane noise, traffic, and everything else.
And be honest, even if you do manage to find a place where you can sit alone and be still, you're there with your smart phone and tablet keeping in touch with the foolishness of the world.
Silence is very disturbing for people. It is the environment of Awakening.
It is the place to hear the heart whispering it's message, that it's 'time to wake up, it's time to live your life, and the world is not the way it is presented to be'.
This is why we really emphasise silence on retreat. Once you surrender into that beautiful and deep place you will meet you, and you will be able to love you and serve you. The moment you know how to love yourself you will intuitively love all beings.
This is the nature of Love.

May all beings be happy.

Staying true to the Path.

When it comes to Dhamma teaching, practice and sharing, I am known as a 'hard liner', principally because I am.

It is true I speak always about Love and share the joy in my heart through stories and jokes, but my relationship to your actual work of being a disciple is simple.

This way of living and being is so beautiful and ultimately so pure that we must commit completely, not to a religious idea, or a guru idea, but to Dhamma itself.

If we truly want to be free from the causes of our fear, unhappiness and discontent we must make the work. There is no other way, and this is exactly what the Master wants to see from their disciples and students. Intention and effort.

Continually making everything easier and more convenient is not the best way to meet the deep habits of the mind and so transcend them.

The equations in Dhamma are always very simple, if you make the practice you will receive the results of making the practice. If you don't do the practice you will receive the results of not making the practice. Simple and clear.

When I trained with my teacher he gave me everything, but one of the most important gifts he gave was his insistence on self reliance. Of do, or don't do.

This simple teaching I share with you now. You are responsible for you and every aspect of your conduct and speech. Take care with what you empower for you cannot avoid its consequences, and remember, I have heard every excuse there is.

Work hard for your own liberation, and if you want to contribute something worthy to the world and all of your relations, let go and let go and let go of the things that cover your loving fearless heart.

May all beings be happy.

Walk on.

Listen to the silence.
When we ourselves become quiet we can hear the silence.
It is an embrace of infinite possibility. It is the sound of Love.
We stand on the edge of an abyss, fearless and without desire, looking into this beautiful emptiness. Here all the answers wait for you.
Didn't you know that there is nothing to get?
Didn't you know that all your efforts ultimately are in vain, and the very thing you search for so desperately in your life is the thing that you already carry with you in every moment?
Love cannot be created nor can it be transformed from something else. Everything is only what it is and is complete in that. Love is love, anger is anger, fear is fear.
Our Dhamma Path therefore is not to create a new 'you', spiritual, knowing and smiling, but simply to allow the old 'you', that collection of fears, anxieties and self justification to fall away and give the space for your fearless loving heart to manifest.
This is the true joy of Dhamma.
There is nothing to get, but everything to do. This is the paradox of authentic Dhamma practice. To be with things as they are, to respond with a loving heart, and never pick up something more to carry. To smile at the day, and walk on.
This is the freedom I speak about.

May all beings be happy.

Meditation and Pure Dhamma.

Our meditation practice is such a beautiful thing, from the elegance of the posture, to the goal of our effort, to be free from the influence of that troublesome part of ourselves that creates difficulties wherever we go.

Self identity or ego is the insidious identification with mind and body as being who and what we think we are. That simple identification can never bring peace, and so through wise reflection and a determined attitude we let go and let go and let go.

And even if you think that your practice is not going well, and your mind is busy thinking and reliving the day, or dreaming, fantasizing and falling asleep, at least you are not out in the world, harming other beings, or causing pain and misery.

You are here, sitting beautifully like a Buddha, still and elegant, surrendering to the simple discipline of our practice, to live with love and be aware, and allowing the universe to unfold naturally.

This is the way to hear the heart, to let go of the Mara mind, and put down the burden we struggle through life with. Now we can bring the gift of our selfless self to all our relationships.

May all beings be happy.

The mind, Dhamma and integrity.

I am always in a state of deepest gratitude for meeting the Buddha, the Dhamma and the Sangha in my life. It was, and is a blessed association, but due to my own kamma and the guidance of my teacher, Sayadaw Rewata Dhamma, I was able to leave Buddhism behind and become one with the direct teachings of the Buddha and of the Pure Dhamma.

Buddhism is a religion that exists in the world and has millions of followers.

Buddha Dhamma are the teachings given by a fully awakened being to take others to full realisation. It is a path that exists only to serve all beings.

The difference between the two is enormous. The difference between the two is liberation.

When I was a monk I was not permitted to dig in the earth for fear of harming the small beings that live there. However, I could allow others to dig in the earth on my behalf!

When I was a monk I was forbidden to take the life of other beings, although I could eat meat from animals killed by others (this I never did).

When I was a monk I was not allowed to touch money, but others could buy anything I needed for me.

And so it went on...

In the political world it is the same.

Politicians can create wars, although they themselves do not go to fight.

Politicians can speak about the poor living on almost nothing, and yet they have so much.

Politicians can manipulate anything and everything to suit their own ideas, but call out others for attempting to reveal the truth.

When Pure Dhamma and its integrity is lost, we enter the world of the mind. Of greed and hatred, of power and possession, and so, when love is lost, manipulation begins.

Not to be deluded or overwhelmed by fear is the beginning of freedom, for it is always your fear that holds you prisoner.

Without fear, you cannot be a victim to life or the manipulations of others.

Reflect, if they have nothing that you want how will they have power over you?

So now we come to the line in the sand.

Who can stand in front of this and say,

"Not me!

I do not kill, nor do I encourage others to kill.

I do not take things that are not mine, nor do I encourage others to take things that do not belong to them.

I do not manipulate fellow beings, nor do I encourage others to manipulate fellow beings.

I do not speak in cruel or harmful ways, nor do I encourage others to speak in cruel or harmful ways.

I do not escape reality through the use of drugs, nor do I encourage others to escape reality through the use of drugs."

This is my Path. This is my integrity. This is my Dhamma.

May all beings be happy.

The truth will always find you.

When I was nineteen years old I lived, worked and meditated in Cardiff, the capital city of Wales in the United Kingdom.
I was training in Transcendental Meditation whilst writing and performing songs with my closest friend Trevor, as a duo called Sparrow. We were well received around the town and all in all, this was a formative and quietly exciting time in my life.
My girlfriend of those days and I worked quite close to each other and she would often come to meet me in the evening so we could walk home together.
On one summer afternoon she arrived unannounced just as I was preparing to go with a friend from work on his motorcycle. The bike would not start so we had to push it and then jump on. Just as we were pushing the bike along the street I saw my girlfriend standing on the opposite side of the road waiting for me. Our eyes met, but I ignored her, and we jumped on the bike as it roared into life and rode off through the streets of Cardiff.
Some hours later I met my girlfriend and she was furious.
She screamed at me saying that I had ignored her and gone off with my friend.
"No," I said," I didn't see you."
"Of course you did, you looked right into my eyes," she yelled.
"No, honestly, I didn't see you."
And so it went on until I persuaded her to accept the lie that I had created that I hadn't seen her.
However, so convincing was this lie that eventually I too believed that I hadn't seen her.
Although this simple incident was never an important story in my life l carried the lie with me for more than twenty years.
However, the more I became a dedicated disciple of Dhamma and practised earnestly every day, the more the past began to arise until one moment in my daily meditation, the clear and honest

memory of that particular event returned.

Of course I had seen her. I looked straight into her eyes. I saw her bewilderment as I turned away and jumped onto the motorcycle with my friend. I deliberately ignored her so that I could do what I wanted to do, and then to save my own 'honour' lied directly to her face.

I had created a fantasy where I could regard myself in a good light, but eventually the truth caught up to me. Of course it did because this is the nature of honest Dhamma practice, to create the space for the meeting of truth. Our truth, the one we often don't want to see.

No matter how intelligent, conniving and persuasive we are, we cannot escape the truth and sooner or later we will have to meet it and accept the reality of what we had empowered.

So the teaching is always simple, don't wait twenty years for a moment of realisation to arrive, but live with honesty and integrity right now.

What we meet in our meditation is ourselves and here, in the silence of loving acceptance, there is nowhere to hide.

May all beings be happy.

The emptiness of self.

We build a life and an identity on a base without substance and because of that we suffer. Self always suffers, it is inevitable, and so the less self identity there is the less suffering there is. Simple, but not easy as not only do we like 'self' we also like our suffering, because it supports our delusion that 'self' is real and permanent.
It is true that 'self' is real, it is just not real in the way you think and then hold on to.
Do you understand?
The equations in Dhamma are always simple and clear. Live from Love and your life becomes loving, live from fear and your life becomes fearful. Who is it that cannot understand that?
This is the Awakening to truth and the profound understanding that the world we experience is the world that we are creating for ourselves moment after moment. No one has power over you, they simply activate your past story and so you react. It's subtle, it's uncomfortable, but it's all a delusion!
'Self' is a flowing river with many turns and bends, rapids and gentle areas, but nothing ever static. This is what we have to understand for the peace and harmony we seek in our ordinary life. There is nothing that you really are, no fixed way you have to be, and so we can flow and respond to different moments without getting stuck in one or another and then attempting to make the whole universe fit around it.
Of course, in the conventional world of work, relationships and culture, we must play the game of life by the rules prescribed, or become monks, nuns or hermits and live away from others.
In our ordinary daily life with its divisions, hierarchy and privilege we will always meet difficulties as we continually crash into the minds of other un-awakened beings, each fighting to hold on to their own 'self identity'.
How can there ever be peace in such a place.

So, as disciples of Dhamma we take the position of living in the world and yet not being part of the world, and so to be open to the reality that no matter how difficult things may seem, everything is the gift in front of us.

To stay on our Path and continue to advance we only need to stay alert to the endless demands of 'self' to be acknowledged and accepted as valid and valuable. 'Self' is always a liar, and will drag us down by the ankles if we allow it to. You're fine, you're really fine. Fighting to be better is just more 'self' following the old storyline that you're not good enough and you'll never make your parents happy.

When we are free from 'self', we are free from the difficulties this delusion brings.

No more internal fighting and struggle, but the simple flowing with life as it manifests moment after moment, responding from the heart with love, first for ourselves and then for all beings. Love begins with you, it is the protection we need from self, and that's what self hates! Even 'self' cannot survive in the face of Love.

The world then is a place we visit to shop, drink coffee and work, but not more than that and when the noise is too loud we must leave.

This is the Way of the heart. This is the Dhamma.

May all beings be happy.

Happiness is our common human goal.

No matter how we may speak about it or whatever specific names we give it, it is always the driving force of our lives.

It is the voice inside our head, continually talking, continually planning and, without the balance of wisdom, continually convincing us to follow the same old ways.

As long as we don't understand the endless momentum of the 'happiness delusion', we will always be victims to it. Chasing one idea, one hope and one dream after the next. Looking, wishing and even praying for the perfect person, the perfect job and ultimately, perfect happiness in the perfect life. This quest is endless and the most direct and realistic way to see the reality of this particular truth is to look at our own lives. After all these years we are still seeking, still shopping, still acquiring.

When will we ever have enough? When will all the conditions for the happiness we seek ever be fully present in our lives?

Until we understand the impermanent nature of happiness we will always be pursuing it! We cannot with any certainty, make it arrive in our lives, and we cannot make it stay once it has arrived. It is fragile, delicate and inconsistent, but this is the nature of happiness.

However, because we do not understand the impermanent nature of happiness we struggle to hold onto it and consequently battle with life and everything that it contains.

At some point in our training we have to realise this ultimate truth; happiness is happiness, but happiness is suffering!

However, real happiness, true happiness, perfect unconditioned happiness is always already present in our life, just waiting for us to re-connect with it.

This is the natural condition of the mind. In reality there is nothing to do and nothing to get. Our Dhamma work therefore is to simply let go of the obstacles that cover this happiness and so become whole again. To simply be.

We need to let go of our habit of judging, criticising and complaining and trying to control everyone and everything and simply be with the conditions as they are. Everything is arising and passing away, this is the nature of life and the universe. The moment that we truly harmonise with this fundamental truth, we will meet the perfect happiness of wisdom and love. Understanding, accepting and responding spontaneously moment after moment with the naturally manifesting enlightened mind. For all of us, no matter who we are or where we come from, this is the best gift that we can give ourselves. Unconditional happiness through an aware and loving heart. However, people don't really want what is best, they want what is easiest!

Love, compassion, peace and tolerance are the best, for ourselves and then by extension for all beings in the world.

Anger, hatred, fighting and killing, much more abundantly found in the world will always be the easiest for the untrained mind.

So as Dhamma students we must ask ourselves, 'what is our Dhammic goal?'

'Are we focused on the heart of Love and compassion in our life, and are we really brave and strong enough to want only the best?'

The greatest gift that we can give ourselves and the world is wisdom and this can only ever manifest as peace, love and happiness.

So the Dhamma Path is simple, choose the best – and be truly happy.

May all beings be happy.

Why would we be angry with the teacher?

Meeting the Buddha was perhaps the greatest and most important moment of my life.

Hearing the teachings of Love and Awareness opened my heart to the possibility of putting down my fears and bringing something of value not only to myself, but to all beings.

Establishing that practice then with my own teacher of Dhamma under the simple yet deeply profound conditions of application and self responsibility, was everything to me.

The moment the Master says, 'don't believe a single word I say, but investigate for yourselves whether it is true or not' (Kalama Sutta) you will know that you are hearing the voice of absolute confidence in truth.

Belief is not the Path. Direct experience of truth is the Path.

However, as any earnest disciple will tell you, this Path of truth, of continually turning inwards to the subtle cause of any and all our difficulties, demands a fearless nature, a brave heart and a resolve to let go of excuses and finger pointing, and arrive at the heart of the matter, the escape from the delusion of 'self'. The question is never really, 'why do I suffer?' but more, 'when does 'I' suffer?'

When life does not give us what we want it is very easy to blame others. To take our worldly 'self' based position and condemn them for their failures.

However, when we arrive in front of the Master with our problems and complaints, they will always lovingly turn us back to ourselves. To look inside, not outside. Why do we suffer, why do we meet this frustration and how can we be free from our fear? If I can quote my own teacher of twenty two years saying anything to me it would be, 'ah Michael, now you need loving kindness.' He never indulged any fantasies that my unhappiness was somebody else's fault, but turned my head always to the path of Wisdom and

Love.

After that moment of Pure Dhamma instruction it was left for me to apply it to my life and see if it worked or not - of course, it always did.

But believing in the teachings when life is comfortable and applying them during difficulties is not the same thing, and so often, even in the presence of the Master, we don't want to hear the truth of Dhamma, but to have our worldly position supported. The Master can take no place in this. Truth is truth whether we agree with it or not. Our journey then, is to put down the world and its consequent suffering, no matter how appealing it may seem in different moments, and face the Dhamma - our Path to freedom.

It is said that 'when we face the Dhamma, what can go wrong?'

When we turn away from the truth, we cannot be surprised to find ourselves angry with the teacher, who cares only for our liberation.

They may listen with compassion, but they cannot be fooled by argument and politics.

This is the gift of this special and most precious relationship.

May all beings be happy.

Simplify, simplify.

Dhamma understanding and worldly understanding are often exact opposites of each other.
In the world we collect and hold on to as many things as possible, seeking our security in them. Not only material things, but people, relationships, ideas, beliefs, concepts about ourselves and the universe we are part of. We attempt to feel secure by controlling our immediate and then global environment. It is no wonder we meet frustration and disappointment time and time again as we see our hopes and aspirations fall apart as the universe goes its own way and pays no attention to our gross or subtle desires.
The Dhamma life is a beautiful simplicity and based in the understanding of a fundamental truth; nothing is ours!
We don't own anything or anyone and our security lies in harmonizing with this impersonality of the universe and feeling ourselves to be part of the whole, rather than outside attempting to control and manipulate it.
Reflect, if we don't own this very mind and body that we call 'ours', how can we own anything else?
We are in relationship with everything, but we don't own anything.
Beings are the way they are. However that is, we have to accept. We may not like them or their behaviour, but freedom lies in accepting reality, then responding wisely.
We may want them to be different, but that very thought is the first part of our suffering.
The true disciple then uses life as the teacher and lets go of seeking any kind of lasting happiness that is dependent upon the behaviour of others.
Instead we celebrate this life as the wonderful opportunity for Awakening, for without our suffering, how could we end our suffering?
The Dhamma Path is demanding, because it is about letting go of

the cause of our unhappiness in life, and that cause, no matter how we may resist these next few words, is always ourselves.

So, whenever we struggle, if we have the wherewithal to investigate the cause of the pain we feel, we can find a quiet place and simply ask ourselves this question; 'in this moment, what am I attached to?'

The answer will always be the same, that 'it shouldn't be like this!' And there is your suffering.

Acceptance of reality, whether gross or subtle is the first step into liberation. We must smile at life and move on, one step after another.

May all beings find the true Path of liberation from the limitations of 'self'.

May all beings be happy.

The necessity of training alone.

For the seven years before I met Sayadaw Rewata Dhamma my teacher and greatest Dhammic influence in my life, I trained alone. I had practised Transcendental Meditation like so many of my generation, read everything I could find about the Buddha and Buddhism and become a student of both Rinzai and Soto Zen. These different disciplines served me well, but after a series of minor but life changing events, I found myself returned to my small island (Isle of Man) living alone in spiritual isolation.

However, I had the practice of meditation and three books of Buddhist teachings from a Buddhist monk I would later meet, the beautiful Hamalawa Saddhatissa, and so with nothing left to do, I sat every day for half an hour.

Of course there were so many times when there seemed to be no future in my sitting, and many times I resigned myself to giving up, but everyday I would find myself back on my cushion, often complaining to myself about the futility of what I was doing.

However, this way of isolated training stood me in good stead and prepared me eventually for meeting my teacher.

Training alone is difficult but cultivates determination and eventually our own voice in sharing what we have understood. Of course, perhaps it is unnecessary to say that this understanding needs to be later confirmed by a Master of Dhamma.

Jesus spent forty days and nights in the desert in isolation whilst the Buddha trained without a teacher for six years in the forest of Uruvela, so in retrospect I was in good company.

We need to be quiet to hear our heart and in this deep silence we can allow our own ideas and fantasies simply fall away until all that is left is the truth.

When there is no one to listen to, support or argue with our ramblings as we try to make reality coherent, the greatest gift we can give ourselves is to go back into the simple, unambitious form of 'sitting just to sit'.

When I reflect upon my life I see that every part, from the smallest to the greatest, has been a blessing. 'Without this, that could not have happened. Without that, this would not be here now...'

This is the true understanding of Dhamma.

No quick fix. No magic formula. No super deity to save us. Only the silent sitting alone with this being that we call 'self'. Here are all the answers to the deepest and most profound questions, but to receive them we must be quiet and still.

Offered with humility.

                May all beings be happy.

The legacy of training.

Some years ago I was interviewed by a journalist for a modern spiritual magazine.
Usually I decline such things as I seem to be so far away from the popular understanding of 'spiritual' practice and am often confused by what is considered real training.
However, I answered her questions as best I could and was surprised when she exclaimed towards the end of our time together, "wow, you're really radical!"
When I was an adolescent I was afraid of life. Everything disturbed me and it seemed that there was always an ongoing battle to control my environment so I would feel secure. Of course, it was never really effective for me in the same way as it is never really effective for anyone else.
Then I met meditation. Then I met a Master. Then I met the training. Then I met me.
These things became my life and I quickly saw the value of surrendering into the practice rather than continually trying to make things more comfortable for myself.
The notion of quick fixes, instant enlightenment, certificates and personal prestige never occurred to me, and I was simply and lovingly instructed to 'do the work'.
To sit with the mind. To be accepting of what it presented and to let go of my attachment to it as being who and what I am.
I was told not to believe anything, but to test the words of the Masters. To deconstruct the notion of self identity and not construct another one simply to replace it.
In my final meeting with my Master, a Burmese Buddhist monk, with whom I trained for almost twenty three years, he said, 'Michael, I have never tried to teach you Buddhism, only Dhamma'.
I travel and teach and lead courses and intensive retreats because

of his explicit instruction to me to do that. The reason, so that others can benefit by hearing the Dhamma, and putting into practice the teachings of liberation.

None of this part of my life was ever to be about me, only the sharing of Dhamma.

So now, and for the past thirty seven years, I share my training with others. On our retreats you are instructed to sit in silence, to move slowly and elegantly, and make every moment a moment of training. Whether you are sitting, standing, walking or lying down, and every possible variation of those things. Not to follow the mind but to be one with it. To be at peace with it.

To allow the self identity to fall away and let the heart, that fearless loving part of you, to open and manifest into your life.

I don't understand how any of this can be called radical.

It is only the way I was trained by a loving caring Master. It is now only what I share with my disciples.

Often people from other styles of training disagree with me, but life is the true test of the depth of our practice. Sooner or later we will meet the consequence of our deepest wisdom, or persistent delusion.

Offered with humility.

May all beings be happy.

The pain of jealousy.

However we can explain, rationalise, justify and discuss the feeling called jealousy it doesn't help us.

Jealousy comes from fear. The fear that in some way we are not good enough and so will be replaced or ignored by others. This fear based insecurity creates a world of self fulfilling and self destructive fantasy and we can easily become lost in it. Of course, it's all a dream and the things that are important in our life are only important because we make them important.

Do you understand? It's all an empty story and the way out is Love.

This cannot be a surprise. Of course when I speak of Love I do not speak about a conventional romantic or emotional relationship with another, but a relationship with yourself based in acceptance and non judgement.

The mind presents a story and the moment we accept it as only a story it has no power, and so the secret to freedom is ultimately not to mind.

To accept what the mind presents, acknowledge it, smile at it if you can, and do the next thing on your agenda.

Make a cup of tea, wash the dishes, call a friend. With this attitude everything will fall into balance and you will be happy and share that happiness with all beings.

This however can be a lifetimes process and so patience and commitment are necessary.

Do what you do with love and let everything else go.

These are only outlines of what is necessary to be in peace, but perhaps they are useful to fellow travellers on the Path.

May all beings be well and happy.

Dhamma practice when sick.

Many people accept illness as the perfect reason to take a break from practice, but this would not be our Dhamma way.

To sit with the body through unpleasant feelings and often the misery of illness is perfect practice provided we understand how to do it properly.

The most important thing is to take the attitude of just doing it.

Don't look for a special reason or think you have to cultivate a special attitude in advance, just take the posture most comfortable for you and surrender. Let go of any desire or ambition to change something uncomfortable into something better. This is not the purpose of what we do.

Let the attention naturally select an object and rest with that. As the awareness becomes more pronounced the objects will become more subtle.

In our usual sitting practice we use the touch sensation of breath in the nostrils to begin, however, if there is a temporary reason why this is not possible we should use whatever sensation presents itself to us.

Sometimes we can just sit with the absolute misery of an illness and simply allow the awareness to move to wherever there is a natural attraction, other times, as in the case of a head cold or flu, we can place the awareness in the mouth and feel the sensation in the regular movement of breath there.

To be with the body in all its phases is how to understand the Path to liberation properly. If we continually choose one state over another we will never transcend the limitations that we place upon ourselves.

Sit with what is, and don't make excuses. In this way we can always expect good results.

May all beings be happy.

Tired of the world.

When the Buddha described disillusionment with what was perceived as ordinary life two thousand six hundred years ago in India, he called it 'world weariness.' The feeling of deep fatigue as we perceive the emptiness of a life style that has been conditioned into us as having value.

In Dhamma training in all that time of course nothing has changed and as disciples of Dhamma we find ourselves becoming tired of the routine of everyday life and the endless chasing after the things we have been told are important.

We often find ourselves busier and busier but never further ahead in our pursuit of peace or happiness. Sometimes it feels as though we borrow more and more money, simply to pay off what we already owe.

The balance then comes from understanding the expression, 'to live in the world and not be part of the world.'

The potential to live without attachment to the things that ultimately disappoint, but still be a part of life itself.

Life is not suffering, but it is unsatisfactory as long as we grasp at those things that cannot be held. The loving Dhamma teaching is always the same, let go, let go, let go, not to the thing itself, but only to the attachment.

It is attachment that fuels the unsatisfactoriness and desire that fuels the intention.

To live in the world and be free from its entanglement is the promise of Dhamma.

When the Buddha awakened a smile arrived on his lips, the same smile waits for you the moment you put down the belief that this world can ever fully satisfy.

May all beings be happy.

Karaoke spirituality.
When style and tradition is more important than Dhamma.

Often it seems to me that true Awakening and so absolute liberation from greed, hatred and delusion is lost to the popular world. Perhaps it has always been like this, but there are so many people claiming to be teachers now of so many traditions and styles, advocating 'our way' or 'this way', but each singing someone else's song. They may know how to repeat the foreign and exotic words, some may even know the melody but none have the true music.

To be continually speaking about Zen or mindfulness, Buddhism or meditation as vehicles for liberation shows we are still caught in the world of loss and gain, advantage and disadvantage, always promoting or selling something to protect ourselves from our own insecurity in one way or another. It is this world that continues to manifest as the suffering, doubt and disappointment of self identity.

If you are a spiritual or religious teacher of something, right now look at your instinctive feeling about the former statement!

Where there is self there is suffering. Where there is self there is ideology and preference, division and group allegiance and competition.

Talking in an expert way about spiritual things does not necessarily mean you have any depth of true understanding and making your life a business around these things only corrupts that which has real value.

Because attachment to self identity is the obstacle, it is self and its million manifestations that must be let go of, until that time we simply sell our intellectual and emotional positions and dance around the edge of truth, rather than sharing our heart and our selfless nature. We are still asleep in our life, but only now in a different bed.

As the Zen Master Ziyong said, 'when you are in the dream, you still speak the language of dreams'.

People don't usually want to suffer but most it seems are unprepared to let go of the true cause. To be seen as someone who knows rather than simply manifesting that knowing in a beautiful discreet way is still the trap of self.

Truly offered with humility.

                May all beings be happy.

Do I really have to have Love for all beings?

If you want to be in peace in life, you must cultivate a loving relationship with all beings. This simply means to accept the reality of the other as they are in this moment, and then respond. It does not mean that you must like them or approve of their actions, and it most certainly does not mean that you should ever allow anyone to exploit, abuse or take advantage of you in any way!Beings are the way they are, that is their choice - you are the way you are, and that is your choice.

Like so many people, you carry an idea of 'niceness', and this becomes your weakness. You need to let go of the idea that you can only be loved, liked or accepted when you please everyone and put yourself at the end of an imaginary list of importance.

Remember, Loving Kindness begins with you. If you don't have it for yourself, how can you share it with others. Love is your strength, not niceness or being 'a pleaser.' Even the Buddha (and me, and my teacher) was criticised, and so no matter what we do we will always be viewed through the personal lenses and emotional filters of others and their story - in the same way that you do exactly that. No-one sees the world (or events) as it is, we only see it as we are, therefore the less of the past we carry, the less corrupt is our understanding of the moment.

Life is not a test or even a learning ground and the idea that things happen to us personally to reveal something is really just a 'New Age' way to regard situations, that everything occurs to teach us something. Actually life is just happening and we are caught up in it. We follow our old habits and meet the same results or we open our heart, change our habits and meet different results.

In every event, personal or public, gross or subtle, large or small, Love, the unconditional acceptance of the reality of this moment, will always serve you. Then you will respond to what is actually happening, rather than your old story superimposing itself onto

the moment and directing your reaction through fear.
When fear is ended, there is peace.
This is the reason why you need to cultivate an open and loving heart.

> May you and all beings be happy.

The moments of no self.

We cannot say that there are moments of no self, only that there are moments of non attachment to a self identity. When 'you' are not there everything is exactly as it should be. When 'you' are there so many things to be changed.

However, the reality is that 'self' needs support, it needs fear and desire to sustain it and that is why Awakening, however we like to think of it, is simply the dropping away of this attachment.

The moment we intuitively realise that desire can never be fulfilled and fear can never be neutralised by 'self' we will have understood the First Noble Truth, that every experience, even fear and desire, is ultimately unsatisfactory.

Dhamma is the Truth of reality, and so the only thing that has value. Everything else can be said to be a lie and so life itself is dishonest, only a story to hold us in place.

When we realise that we don't need the story, we are free and life is no longer a battle to be won or lost, or a series of compromises to make. True success is peace in the heart and a simple smile into the storm arriving so often until 'self' is released.

But remember, it is only the attachment we have to release, and this attachment is nothing more than holding onto a dream. In that moment (which we spontaneously meet many times a day) everything is exactly as it should be and life is experienced as a flowing harmony.

Our deepest practice then is to recognise the mind as the liar it is and to naturally allow its foolishness to arise and pass away, simply being aware but not paying too much attention.

Offered with my greatest love, respect and humility.

May all beings be happy.

I am turning on the light, where does the darkness go? (Zen koan)

What is known as Dhammic Love, is the absolute freedom in life simply because it is the antithesis of fear. These two aspects of the mind cannot exist at the same time in the same place and of the two, love is always better.

Fear is always about losing something. Something material or more subtly some kind of personal credibility - hence the expression, 'what will people think?'

Who are these people whose opinion we are so afraid of, and why do we even care what views others may have formed of us?

When you have no fear, who has any power over you, can manipulate or control you? In this place you can be true to your highest integrity and accept not only the responsibility of your actions, but also the impersonal consequences of them.

Fear, then is always our weakness and no matter how much we can explain it to ourselves and others, it will never bring a good result in our life.

However, it is important to say that although fear is not our friend, we should at the same time take care with our decisions and actions. Being reckless also may not bring a good result and so balance is important.

To consider each possibility from a mature and open standpoint rather than being frozen through fear or impulsive through recklessness.

An open and loving attitude to life then, is much healthier in every way and will bring good results emotionally, spiritually and physically.

Love transcends liking and disliking and serves all beings equally. It looks for nothing in return and so does not belong to the world of business and emotional politics.

It is the greatest and most beautiful power in life because it is independent of external influences.

In the end, the definition of Love is the acceptance of the universe as it manifests in this moment without applying personal fear based conditions. Then we can respond wisely rather than simply reacting.

The whole of Dhamma, however intellectually and scholarly we may speak about it is extremely simple, 'live with love and be aware.'

This Path is very difficult and that is why so few attempt to follow it. But for those who do and commit to this journey the consequence is great. More peace, joy and happiness in your life at the expense of fear, anxiety and stress. This life then is better for you and all beings.

May all beings be happy.

Going past the past.

When we are together as a group or when you visit me in my room, I can honestly say that my interest is not in whether you agree with me or not but only that you reflect upon my words.

In all these years of sharing Dhamma I have never felt that my position is to convince you that I'm right and you should blindly follow everything I say, but only that you should take responsibility for yourself and accept the consequences of the delusions you carry and then manifest into the world.

Understanding life and Dhamma is a subtle and often uncomfortable process as we let go more and more of the conditioning and belief systems we have been exposed to, often arriving at the question, 'When everything has been let go of, who and what are we?'

This common and fearful thought is the obstacle to the very liberation you seek.

In the end, in every aspect of life, you are alone with yourself and cannot help but meet the consequence of continually empowering and reinforcing the delusions you carry. The result of this simply becomes deeper and more stubborn delusions.

So we take our meditation posture, still peacefully and allow our old story to run out. We see it, accept it for what it is, and let go of our emotional attachment to it as being who and what we are.

You will not disappear and you will not forget your life, but you will release the pain that comes from reliving the same moments over and over.

This, then is the freedom I speak about. Not from the world, but the conditions that make the world - your unique and personal world.

This is worth your greatest effort.

May all beings be happy.

Everything is Dhamma.

When we seek stability in our life it is often a shock to discover that it doesn't actually exist.

How can that be true when we've been told so many times that it is real and needs only the right person, the right job, the right education, etc.

But nothing is stable and a simple look at our own life will confirm it and that it's not only you whose life is spinning, meeting change after change after unrelenting change. It's everybody because it is the nature of things.

Our happiness, peace and contentment then lies in wisely surrendering into what is often perceived as chaos and responding with integrity. Keeping our authenticity and doing that which needs to be done.

When we face the Dhamma we will see that everything is teaching us. The hard lessons, the painful lessons and the joyful lessons, all part of the simple reality of life.

There is no Father Christmas, there is no tooth fairy and there is no stability to be found anywhere.

The moment we intuitively understand and accept this, we are free. Free from the mind screaming 'it shouldn't be like this.' Free to act in a pure way, putting down a destructive self interest and sharing our love and our understanding with the world.

Old age, sickness and death are not punishments meted out to only a few unfortunates, but the reality of this thing we call life. And in the end they are our greatest teachers.

May all beings be happy.

The need for silence.

Silence is always an important part of our Dhamma training as it presents the perfect environment for the cultivation of a focused mind and the consequential awareness.

It is an absolutely essential part of our correct discipline on retreat. We can speak about four aspects of silence beginning with the most gross form of simply not speaking. To break our habit of communicating every thought, mood, feeling and emotion regardless of its value. This includes to refrain from silently mouthing words at the breakfast table or whispering.

The second aspect is not to communicate with others through eye or any kind of physical contact. Although these contacts may remain non verbal the often misunderstood signals from another can be distracting from the simple instruction of turning our attention inside and resting it upon ourselves.

We can easily find ourselves drawn out into a misconceived understanding of another person on retreat, becoming emotionally involved in what we see.

Crying, which can happen occasionally on retreat, is not always from distress and so it is better for our own journey, in these special circumstances, not to become involved.

The third aspect is to move slowly and elegantly wherever we are, either with the group or alone in our room, and not allow the old habits of mind to dictate our behaviour.

As the daily tensions leave our body through our silent and self contained behaviour we naturally become slower and more beautifully precise in all our movements, how we sit, how we stand, how we eat and every other aspect of movement. When the mind is in peace the body responds with elegance.

The fourth and highest aspect of silence has the Buddhist name of Citta Viveka - the silent mind. This is when the experience of the mind is so vast and peaceful (having not continually stimulated it through not adhering to the other aspects of silence), that everything can arise and pass away free from our habit of grasping or rejecting.

Here we are at peace with everything the mind presents and can allow the Path of purification (Visudhimagga) to safely and harmlessly release our old story into the emptiness of the universe. You don't disappear, only the old kammic habits of thinking and behaving in well established styles fall away and so no longer influence this present moment.

However intelligent and creative you may be on true Dhamma retreats, you cannot escape the limiting consequences of not developing a deep and love based silence.

May all beings be happy.

Understanding Dhamma freedom.

However much we may argue for them, the obstacles to our complete freedom are desire and fear.

We have to understand that what belongs to the body belongs to the body and what belongs to the mind belongs to the mind.

Food, water, shelter and clothing as protection from the elements and medicine in times of sickness. These are the four requirements and are necessary for the body to maintain its ability to continue on the Path to Awakening. They are simple and enough.

Desire and fear belong to the mind.

It is desire that continually makes us reach for more because we feel that what we have is never enough and it is fear that leads to holding on so tightly to what we have in case we lose it. Before Awakening these movements of mind are endless and can never lead to peace.

When the desire for meat has fallen away, no matter how great the chef, the plate is not interesting for you.

When the desire for sexual contact has fallen away, no matter what the presentation it is intuitively and wisely understood as empty. When there is no grasping at any form of happiness outside yourself, you are free.

To be free from desire and fear is the true and ultimate liberation as both always belong to self. The true obstacle to your freedom therefore is attachment to a self identity and the delusion it empowers to constantly reinforce itself.

Liberation is realised when self is finished and the teaching is always the same, let go, let go, let go.

May all beings be happy.

The love of suffering

People love to be offended. Just notice how sensitive you are in your relationship with the world. It doesn't take much, a glance, a word, a gesture, an action almost anything can be a reason and an excuse to make your claim to be offended.

Of course that's never the reality of the situation, but what we really like is to make our life dramatic! To believe others have an intention to upset us, so we can take the part of the victim in our own story, and so justify our suffering. Suffering is always dramatic and an empowerment of self identity, happiness is simply a lightness of being and a smile on the lips.

Actually if we just stayed in our spiritual and emotional centre we would recognise the truth, that others can't offend us, but we can always take offense - at anything.

That others don't ever have the power to hurt us only we can do that, and that no one can break our heart only we can do that.

The moment we put down our addictive attraction to the drama of life we will recognise our own power, and so be free from the fantasy of mind and its consequent suffering.

The world that you experience is the one that you create for yourself moment after moment, and no matter how strongly you can blame others and point your finger, you are responsible for the quality of your relationship to the moment, and so only you can change it.

Between suffering and happiness, happiness is better.

Be stronger than your old story.

May all beings be happy.

The subtlety of separation.

Speaking as a Buddhist, as a Muslim, as a Hindu, as a Christian, as a housewife, as a teacher, as a man, as a woman, as a vegetarian, as a vegan, as a carnivore, as a doctor, as a musician, as a fan, as a sportsman, as a sportswoman, as a German, as an American, as a Frenchman, as a socialist, as a conservative, as a boss, as a common worker, as a gay man, as a gay woman, as a feminist...

Every time we begin a thought or sentence in this way we subtly separate ourselves from the universe and all other beings by empowering yet another transient identity.

We create an environment for superiority and a world that is unique and personal to us, but of course it's all a delusion because in reality there is nothing that you really are and no way you have to be.

Creating and then holding on to an apparent identity can only lead to unhappiness and dissatisfaction as, over time and association with people identifying themselves in the same way, you still find yourself alone, with your own unique views and opinions based on this now shared and fragmented identity.

Freedom does not lie in the superficial security of belonging to a group or of becoming someone or something that gives you a place in life, but rather the opposite, of letting go of all limitations and being the true no-person that you truly are.

May all beings be happy.

The beauty of Love.

Love is the gift we bring to ourselves and the whole universe. When we love truly we accept the other without conditions. We make no demands that they behave in a particular way simply to please us.

We do not try to control or manipulate them but treat them with respect and kindness accepting them as they are.

We do not seek perfection in the other, but allow the space for them to feel free and to show their own heart, in this way they are already perfect.

With love for ourselves we respond to their behaviour with compassion and wisdom, doing what we need to do to guard our own integrity and sense of well being.

This means to love truly.

When two or more beings enter a relationship in this way they each bring something of real value, they bring the best part of themselves. That part that will serve the other, that part that will care for the other, that part that will protect the other and never ask for something in return.

Love is more than a kiss, it is an acceptance without conditions.

Love is more than an embrace, it is a commitment to serve.

Love is more than a feeling, it is the manifestation of the purest part of you.

To share in the suffering and unhappiness but also to celebrate the joy and success in the world.

In this way, to love one being is to love all beings, and to be intimately connected to the universe and everything it contains.

May you, and all beings be happy.

The truth is not in books.

At one time many years ago my teacher, a very senior Burmese Buddhist monk, was alone in his monastery in England when there was a knock on the door.

Because he was by himself it was he who went to answer it to be met by two well dressed and charming Jehovah's Witnesses. Even though it was a Buddhist monastery and my teacher wore the simple saffron robes of a Buddhist monk, they were not deterred and began their attempt to save his soul.

Of course during the conversation my teacher was able to offer many counter points to their presentation until finally they asked if he would meet with their senior, who would much better explain how he was wrong and they were correct in their religious views. Reluctantly my teacher agreed and half an hour later they arrived again, this time with the third person, a very kind elderly man.

My teacher invited them into the monastery and took them to the library. Here they sat and the conversation began.

After some time my teacher raised his hand to ask a question.

"Please tell me," he began, "how do you know that God is real?"

The senior Jehovah's Witness held up his bible and said, "because this book says he is!"

My teacher gestured to all the books in the monastery's library and replied gently, "but all these books say he is not."

(This story recounted to me some days after the event.)

Truth is not contained in a book. It lives in our heart and however we can justify our actions by telling ourselves that we are serving a greater being, we will, without fail always meet the consequence of our actions.

It is not necessary to cultivate a belief system to be kind, loving, generous and caring, this is already the Way of the heart, but it is a useful excuse to justify every kind of intolerance, violence, social, gender and racist repression and the exploitation and cruelty to animals and fellow human beings. To explain our bias in favour of men, our group, our unkind action towards others because they are different to us.

Conversations about the reality of God always seem to be a huge mis-direction in any relationship as neither side can provide real evidence for or against.

God says this, God says that. The Dhamma position is, what does your loving heart say?

However, it does seem to me that mankind is always able to improve upon gods work by covering hair on women and even the whole body in some cases.

Perhaps I am wrong but I do feel that genital mutilation comes from the mind of men, not God, as with animal torture and sacrifice.

If God is perfect, how can his (or her) work need improving?

So these questions come to nothing in our Dhamma training. You are responsible for you, for your kindness, for your cruelty and for your contribution to the welfare of this planet and everything on it.

Actually, in our Dhamma training the question of God isn't something we need to concern ourselves with.

If we think back to the moment we awoke this morning and trace the events of the day until this moment now we can see that some good things happened, and some not so good things happened, and in any event, things turned out as they did.

Now, if we tell ourselves that God exists, these things happened. If we tell ourselves that God does not exist, these things happened anyway.

Whether God exists or not, does not alter our life in any way, and forming an opinion or taking a position for or against his reality, does not help us on our spiritual quest. The road to liberation must be free from blind faith and belief.

We can only ever know what we know, and keep an open mind about the rest.
However, if we have to cover our faces to do 'gods work' we can be fairly sure that we are deluding ourselves.

>May all beings be happy.

From earnest disciple to Master.

Even if my teacher, for the most noble of reasons insisted that I teach, I was not happy to receive this instruction. However, because of my love and respect for this man and the tradition and lineage we followed, I did it. The rest is history.
What is not known so well is the resentment, jealousy and criticism I often had to endure. People want to be the first, the best, the most important and so often they arrive to hear only their own version of Dhamma spoken in the way they understand and to take a place in front of others. I personally met this many times, often with the unspoken whisper 'it's just Mike from the factory, who does he think he is? or, 'I knew him when he was...'
Even standing next to my teacher I could often feel this rejection.

It is what we meet in the world of unawakened beings, not just in the Dhamma hall or on retreat, but in every aspect of daily life, so what to do?
If our intention is to serve the teacher, lineage and tradition that we honor so much, then we accept the hostility of jealousy and foolish abuse by recognising it's cause. We ourselves however, stay on our Path. Dogs may howl at the moon, but the moon goes about its own way with no regard to the noise below.
For those who know, the Path is clear.
We present the Way as clearly as possible letting go of the idea that others should understand, accept or even appreciate what we say, do or present. We may take care, but we cannot make others see that.
In the end we are all responsible for our own path which takes us to or away from liberation.
The Buddha himself met this, as did my teacher, as did I.
The difference between knowing the mind and simply following the mind is liberation.

So from my love, compassion and concern for all beings, I offer gladly these few words.

In the end we are all free to do anything we feel is correct for each of us individually and we must graciously, openly and lovingly accept that.

However, if we don't awaken in this very lifetime, when will we do it?

Offered with infinite love,

                May all beings be happy.

A moving stillness.

Meditation is a multi significant word. It can mean almost anything we want it to and during many thousands of years so many styles and practices have evolved, each with their own special quality and tendency.

Here we practice a form of meditation popularly called Vipassana. However the name does not define only a sitting and walking meditation practice but much more, an approach and a deep intuitive understanding of life.

When we sit in meditation we are always alone. No matter how many people are in the Dhamma hall with us, we are always alone. Alone with this mind and this body, to the physical aches and pains, the mental boredom, excitement and seemingly endless thoughts, moods, feelings and emotions.

Our way then, is to allow the space to see, know and finally let go of the attachment to these things as being who and what we are.

Although there is a clear structure of our practice there is no specific or precise technique such as mantras, reflections or mentally identifying the thoughts or consciously moving the awareness through the body. When we sit in this stillness we do not create anything extra to obstruct the arising of insight that comes from our personal and intimate experience with the moment that naturally leads to the direct understanding of the true nature of self.

No busy mind avoiding the reality of the moment, but rather the silent peaceful acceptance and realisation that whatever begins must end. Each thought, mood, feeling and emotion is nothing more than a fleeting cloud ultimately empty except for the importance we give it. Only a movement arising from the past to be experienced and lovingly released into the emptiness of the universe, and so an opportunity to be free from its influence.

This is our Way of stillness. Of internal and external stillness.

Fear and desire fall away as the base for their presence no longer exists. We sit without ambition and begin to walk through life bringing that fearless loving stillness into every moment.
This is our practice. This is our Way of loving acceptance. This is Dhamma.

> May all beings be happy.

Questions, questions.

There are many reasons to find and then stay close to a true Master of Dhamma and so it is not necessary to always arrive with a deep and profound question.

There are many other considerations to take into account such as a gentle observation of their behaviour in different situations or simply being in their presence.

However, when there is a question it should be understood that the answer from the teacher is really just a pointer or suggestion as to how you can proceed, but always in the end the work that is necessary to do you must do for yourself. The moment you know, by your own tried and tested experience, there will be no need to ask about it.

Primarily the teacher must show their understanding by a living example and so in every moment show their integrity to stay true to the Path of Dhamma without compromise, and compassion for all beings by radiating Love and kindness in all situations. Simple things in principle, but not always present in the religious or spiritual world.

Eventually all questions from the student will fall away, not because they have fully understood the Path, but because there develops spontaneously an intuitive knowing of what should be done.

All that is left then is a movement in life. A direction to walk, rather than a goal to be achieved, sometimes comfortable sometimes not, but each step inspired by the determination to be true to the highest tenets of Dhamma; to live with love and be aware.

There are wonderful loving and wise teachers in the world but many more who will endlessly encourage your belief that they are indispensable to your spiritual welfare, and so manipulate your sensibilities for their own benefit.

As always, take care with whom you sit in front of.

The biggest questions are the ones you ask yourself; in this situation what needs to be done to restore harmony and balance? What more can I do to truly serve others? How can I help?
Contact with the teacher is important, not because you have a question for him or her, but because they are seen as your reminder and inspiration on the Dhamma Path.

May all beings be happy

Magic Dhamma.

I often say that if I could take away your pain and difficulties in life just by touching your forehead or holding your hand, I would do it without a moments hesitation. But of course I can't do that. I can only share with you my joy, my love and my enthusiasm for Dhamma. To remind you that there is nothing wrong here, it's only suffering. Not pleasant, but not wrong either.

We have to meet our old story. To see it, to know it and to ultimately release our emotional attachment to it as being who and what we are.

Only we can do this work. We can be supported by the teacher of course, but in the end we are alone with this mind. We are always alone.

And even if I could remove your unhappiness simply by a touch or a magic chant, how would it really help you? What would you learn from that?

When our understanding is clear we will see that whatever we experience, pleasant or unpleasant, becomes the doorway to our own Awakening.

This is Dhamma. Far beyond any narrow technique of meditation or cult attraction, but the liberating work that only we can do.

Be with the mind and be peaceful. Allow it to be the gift it really is and just.....let.....go.....

May all beings be happy.

Go beyond the words.

To fully understand Dhamma you must always test the words of the teacher.

Buddha said, Jesus said, God said, means nothing against your own direct experience of truth. You are the architect of your life and it is you who must meet the consequence of the mind states that you empower.

To quote great teachers is fine, but do you understand beyond the words?

True Dhamma practice is not simply picking up new ideas and stock phrases to carry, or identifying yourself with an ancient spiritual tradition, but rather putting down the old story you fill your life with.

Dhamma training is always an unlearning process, to let go of the movements of mind that keep you always facing in the same direction in your life and so always meeting the same consequences of disappointment, frustration and fear.

To go beyond a limited 'self' identity is the Way of Dhamma, to let go, let go and let go, until all that is left is the beautiful loving heart and a smile on the face.

May all beings be happy.

The Dhamma hug.

There are many reasons to keep a close contact with your Dhamma Master.
You may feel that there are practical questions you want to ask, or further instructions necessary for your journey, or perhaps you just need a Dhamma hug.
So many times I would telephone my own Master (many years before internet and modern varieties of communication), just to hear his voice. To be reminded of our relationship. As time went by and my understanding grew, I would struggle to find a question, any question that would merit my call. Eventually there were no questions left, only the need for contact.
But of course he knew my heart and so would lovingly respond with a few words, not about practice, but about my day to day life. "How is your wife, your children, your work. How are you?"
He would speak in a kind and fatherly way and that would be enough to remind me that although I always walk alone on my journey, I am in good company.
Now I endeavour to offer the same companionship and parental love to my own students. What we ourselves receive, we share.
Modern communication is easy, with no need to wait until after six in the evening for low price telephone calls, but now with sound and vision together, we can meet. You will tell me that in one way or another, you suffer and I will tell you it's alright, it's just suffering. It may not be pleasant, but it's alright.
Now you will relax a little, knowing that you too are not alone, and your struggle is understood, that you are not doing anything wrong, but only meeting the consequences of that which has gone before. So, 'chin up', be confident, face the new day and continue, I will be here and you do not disturb me with your questions.
Even if you ask the same one in a variety of ways, it's still the Path, and when all your questions finally fall away you will experience

freedom from the fearful and controlling aspect of mind.
In the end, all Dhamma teaching is a simple reminder to the heart to be gentle, to be patient and to be kind to itself.
Because we often forget this, because we often feel alone on our Path and because we need a hug, the Master waits for you, to support your effort and to remind you that whatever the mind may tell you, this is the most important thing in your life, so take care of you. The Path is not always easy, not always comfortable, not always clear, but always worth your greatest effort.
This is the Way of Love, and this is the Path we walk together.

May all beings be happy.

Disappointment.

Disappointment is the other side of expectation.
Without expectation there can be no disappointment and so the question is, how to live in the world without expectation?
In Dhamma training we are encouraged to cultivate the 'don't know mind' as this is the way to live in the world and harmonise with the ever changing possibilities of life without struggling.
'Not knowing' is the reality of every moment and all beings meet the experience of life changing suddenly because of one, often seemingly innocent moment that they could not have foreseen or prepared for.
So, the idea that everything will work out well or even its opposite, that nothing will go well for us, are in the end, only ideas and aspects of mind based in our own personal ways of thinking. They have no more reality than we give them.
The truth is that we don't know what can happen in the next moment and certainly not in the next five weeks, months or years. Therefore, the 'don't know mind' is our protection against suffering as it aligns us with reality.
So, when we ask what will be the outcome of a particular moment in our future, we can answer with complete honesty, 'I don't know'. Now we can be in peace and allow things to take their natural course. We can interact, do our best for the result we would like, but nothing can ever be guaranteed.
In a universe of infinite possibilities getting what we want is never a sure thing, so relax, you didn't do anything wrong, it's just life.

May all beings be happy.

Always ask how.

If your teacher tells you to 'live with love and be aware', and to 'just let go,' or speaks about your cosmic connection with the 'divine' or other abstract concepts like 'higher self' it is your responsibility to ask the question, 'how?'

"How do I do that?" and to receive a clear answer and direction in your effort to realise freedom.

Nice words and warm feelings whilst you sit in front of the Master will not take you to liberation, however, walking on the Path, step by step, with clear instructions and guidance will.

Giving up your identification with a self identity is no easy task, but if you are guided by someone who has already arrived at liberation and who shares their unconditional Love and council with you, it can certainly be done.

But reflect, if the teacher is not free, what can they share? Their delusions may be more subtle than for others, but delusion is delusion and its consequence in the world ultimately is to be like a one eyed person leading the blind.

We hear many stories of so called Masters abusing their students or engaging in sexual activities, but reflect, when desire and fear are finished where can either of these aspects of mind find a place to hold on to?

If your Master is awakened, what can they possibly want from you? Reflect on this, it's important.

If your Master is awakened, what can they possibly want from you?

The only function of the Master then, is to guide and care for you like a loving parent, clearly stating what needs to be done and what needs to be relinquished for your own liberation, and then how to do it.

They live only to serve others, never for their own glorification. They are quiet and discreet and do not seek fame or fortune, for these things belong to the world. Whether they sit in front of two people or a thousand, the teaching is the same and shared with the love and enthusiasm of someone caring only for the welfare of all beings.

So the message is simple; in a world where spirituality can be translated into an enormous business enterprise, and a path to spiritual fame and wealth, take care of who you put your trust in. All desire and fear, manifesting as manipulation and gamesmanship belong to the world. Love, service and infinite compassion belong to the emptiness of self.

This is the Way of true Dhamma.

May all beings be happy.

Embracing life.

Embracing life is a modern spiritual and New Age expression that is meaningless in Dhamma training.

You are alive therefore you have already embraced life. And if you are ever in a real life threatening situation (such as drowning for example) you will see just how much you have embraced life as you struggle to keep it.

So, we are born and we are alive, now what will we do with this precious gift?

In every moment we have the opportunity to be a Buddha or a demon, to share our beautiful loving heart or to express our fear though greed and selfishness.

The choice is always ours and the more we commit to a true Dhamma Path the less choosing there is. Love, and the sharing of our compassionate heart will always take precedence.

So, let go of meaningless New Age sound bites and give your energy to your own development of Love and Awareness and let everything naturally fall into place.

May all beings be happy.

The obsession with others.

We continually give our power away when we concern ourselves with the way we think others feel about us.

We all would like fair treatment and respect from the world, but often it just doesn't come, even from our own family members we sometimes meet behaviour that is so low, so unkind, that we ask ourselves how is it possible that we could have the same parents? But the world is made up of the dreams and fantasies of the mind and the more we silently insist that everyone in all circumstances behaves in specific ways around us, the more the doors to our suffering open.

Beings are the way they are, that is their choice.

You are the way you are, that is your choice.

Our protection then is Love, first for ourselves and then for all beings.

When the heart is open our boundless, energetic Love manifests as compassion for the world and the beings who often behave so badly, for they will always meet the consequence of the mind states they empower.

It is Love in the end that protects us from the poison of the world and gives us the strength to respond to each situation with whatever action or speech is necessary.

Love may be gentle but never insipid. It is always strong and resilient. Where there is Love, there is no fear, and hence it is called, the fearless state.

Love is the essence of Dhamma.

When the Buddha was insulted by an angry Brahmin on one occasion, he took no offense and later, when asked to explain his mild behaviour he replied, "if someone offers you a gift and you do not accept it, who is left holding the gift?"

The teaching then is simple, though like all true Dhamma teachings, not always easy to apply, do not pick up the gift of

anger, ill will and other forms of poor behaviour and stay true to your own Dhamma heart.
In this way you will guard your happiness and bring the gift of your love to the world.

> May all beings be happy.

The bravery of self responsibility.

That terrible action, no matter what the circumstance, if you did it, you're responsible. Those horrible, hurtful words, no matter what provocation, if you said them, you're responsible. In every moment and in every situation we exist in a universe filled with the possibility for love or hatred.

It is a delusion to think that others have any real power to make you do or say something you don't want to. It is the nature of the subtlety of cowardice to project responsibility onto others, screaming, 'it's your fault, you made me do it!'

In the end, integrity and honesty is everything, so be clear about who and what you are, and never compromise. Accept the result of the mind states you empower and then act upon. Whatever you may think, there is no escape from the consequence of what you bring into your life and the lives of others.

This is why the greatest Masters advise Love, more Love and then even more Love, first for yourself and then for all beings equally and everywhere.

When we empower Love, our life becomes loving, when we empower fear, our life becomes fearful. Who is it that cannot understand the simple law of consequence?

May all beings be happy.

Love means compassion for all beings.

When I was a little boy I spent my summer holidays on my uncles farm on the Isle of Man. I loved it, to be in nature with all the beautiful animals, to care for them and to talk in my simple childish way with them.

Of course I had no concept that they were being raised simply so they could be sold, killed and eaten, but how would I?

Something so preposterous, something so barbaric as that?

But because of that very reasoning, the truth was always hidden from me.

I was told that my 'friends' had gone to a better field or a new home, to have a happier life.

Now reflect, why are a child's feelings protected from the reality of the situation? If something is acceptable in our heart, why hide it from children? Why not simply explain that this being has no rights and no value except to be fattened, sold, killed and eaten?

So I would talk to the cows whilst they were being milked, sing to the pigs and count the sheep every evening to make sure none had roamed out of their fields (it took me years to realise that this was only a device to give me something to do before bed at night, and not necessary at all!)

Eventually I grew up and began to see behind the stories that cover man's endless cruelty to these wonderful animals, and perhaps it was that very deceit that helped shape my Dhamma life?

We each have the potential to live a loving, caring compassionate life, for ourselves and all beings. Sharing our heart and celebrating the value of all the myriad creatures we share our planet with.

Eating the flesh of cruelly murdered animals is not a necessity, only a habit and it can easily be let go of if we reflect on our mutual similarities: We all want to be happy, we all want to feel secure in our life, we all want to avoid pain. That one group or species should ever exploit another does not fit a Dhamma life.

The moment we understand suffering as we experience it for ourselves we can no longer blindly inflict it upon others and we intuitively surrender to the beautiful teaching of Love and compassion of the Buddha;

All beings fear pain and death.
All beings love life.
Remembering that we are one like them,
let no-one harm or kill another.

(Dhammapada vs 130)

Love lives in our heart, and the power to change how we live and share our life with all other beings begins in a moment of true compassion.

May all beings without exception be happy.

Beyond addiction.

Perhaps it is unnecessary to say that Dhammic liberation is freedom from any form of addiction. Gross addictions are easy to identify, strong drugs like alcohol, nicotine and so called recreational drugs like heroin, cocaine and the like are obvious examples but there are more subtle and possibly more limiting addictions that are not so easy to see.

The dependence on the idea that we are right and others are wrong. That we are 'nice' people and that our group, our gender, our religion and social classification are seen to be superior and acknowledged as that. Emotional dependence, to feel loved, to feel appreciated, to feel needed are some simple examples.

But any dependence on something outside ourselves is doomed to failure and so in our Dhamma training we let go of that. We let go of our addictions. We grow up and become adults in the truest sense of the word.

Once we find the courage to completely 'let go' we are free, no longer seeking out happiness and security outside ourselves, but living peacefully and lovingly in a world where we are free and able and ready to respond to whatever presents itself in any moment.

Addictions do not bring peace and however you can argue for them, will always be a barrier to your liberation.

The wise person will be like an island,
independent and secure in their wisdom.
In this way they are sure to attain liberation.

(Dhammapada vs 236)

May all beings be happy.

Practice a lot.

This is a beautiful way to be, to live with love and to be aware, and the first person to benefit is you.
So, 'practice a lot' was the instruction from the Buddha to his disciples, it was the instruction from my teacher to me and it is my instruction to you.
And what we are doing here on retreat is so simple, and often I think that this very simplicity becomes a difficulty for people.
We're not bowing to Buddha statues, or chanting or performing other rites and rituals, in fact we are not doing anything to distract you from you.
So here we meet the truth, the truth of this being called 'self'. What can be more beneficial to the world than that. To dedicate your life to Awakening so that you will be happy and then share that happiness with all beings.
This is the Way of Dhamma as shared by the Buddha under the Bodhi Tree in India two thousand six hundred years ago.
Nothing has changed and the responsibility for your own Awakening lies only with you.

May all beings be happy.

The truth of suffering.

We only suffer when we don't get what we want! It may sound frivolous but it is the reality of our life. We hold on to things after their time and so naturally meet the consequence of that. Our difficulties, no matter how much we can create and maintain a story in our head, is only about that.

One thing we can do, if we consider ourselves to be disciples of Dhamma to support us in a moment of stress or difficulty, is to go to a quiet place where we will be alone and ask ourselves one simple question: 'In this moment, what is it that I am holding on to?'

The answer is always the same and it is: I am holding on to the idea that life and this moment of life shouldn't be like this!

There, right there is our suffering, the rejection of the reality of the moment.

Look, it is like this and it's O.K. It may be painful, but it's still O.K.

Reality is happening all around us in every moment and it's not personal, it's only life unfolding unmoved by personal desires, aversions and whims.

Life is not personal and it's not about you - you only make it about you and that is why it is so easy to get caught up in perceived insults and slights in relationships in life. How we view and experience the world comes directly from us and as it is the same for all living beings, it is no wonder that we don't agree on everything and often fight and argue about an issue that appears to be something so evident that it needs no explanation.

And look at you, you are a fully formed and complete human being. Your potential for happiness is enormous, and only requires one thing from you, to let go of the past and your identification with it.

The whole of our experience of life is about beginnings and

endings, moment after moment after moment, from the grossest to the most subtle, but in every instance we are helpless to make things stable. This moment is already moving away before we can even attempt to hold it. Our Dhamma Path reminds us that it is better to celebrate what we had rather than grieve for what (we think) we lost.

Only we are responsible for our own happiness, so look to be happy yourself, to find the things in life that fulfill you and serve the world with your own love, rather than looking for it from others.

Offered with love for the benefit of all beings.

May all beings be happy.

Facing the Dhamma.

The path is straight, but people love to be sidetracked.
(Tao te Ching verse 42)

The moment I met true Vipassana training and the loving guidance of my Master, I never looked for something else. Even from the first moment I recognised it as the greatest blessing in my life. An untainted way of Love and Awareness leading to the absolute and perfect liberation from the insidious corruption and subsequent suffering of the desire and fear based mind.

Dhamma is already complete and needs nothing added to it, and all the disciple needs to do is stay on the Path. Just one simple thing, do not allow the mind to distract you from the step by step journey to liberation. Each new thing, ceremony or fashion that is added to the purity of practice becomes a pollution and ultimately a barrier to self realisation. After all, it can only be 'self' who is dissatisfied with the intrinsic simplicity of Love and Awareness and everything new we add or pick up merely becomes one more thing we will have to release in the future.

The more we speak about 'self', the more we show our lack of understanding. The more we try to convince others of its value the more we show our frailty. The more we bring it into our lives, the more we wander off the Path.

The Buddha is my great hero, not the mystical being from the legends but the being who showed the smile of ultimate freedom, beyond religion, beyond rites and rituals. This simple and straight Path is available to all men and women who wish to be free. Its only requirement is that we always face the Dhamma and resist the Mara mind of distraction.

Offered with love.

May all beings be happy.

Beyond the delusion of practice.

In my Dhamma life I am happy to be a simple Master, taking care of that which was entrusted to me.

I offer no ceremony, no certificate, no initiation, no ladder to climb in front of others.

I give no reward, no badge of office for your effort in meditation.

I share only my love and enthusiasm for Pure Dhamma, the teaching of Gotama before religion was born.

I encourage honesty and integrity in practice - such a difficult Path to walk when the spiritual business world offers so much.

In the temples and monasteries I see people with their hands together in Anjali all the while pushing for their place in front of others.

I hear people speaking of love and compassion all the while happily eating the flesh of fellow beings.

I hear people speaking of mystical experiences all the while pursuing the lowest aspects of human behaviour.

For me, I have nothing to offer but the silence of meditation and the elegance of Pure Dhamma practice bringing us to the joy of the heart.

Not seeking to be someone, but aspiring to be no one is the Way of Pure Dhamma, and those who arrive with humility and right intention will always find a place next to me.

May all beings be happy.

The Dhamma quest.

What you seek is the same as everyone, and that is certainty in life.
The belief in the superficial equation that 'if I do this I will get that.'
Sometimes it works the way we would like and other times not at all, and then everything else in between. In other words, certainty does not exist in the conventional world, and so we struggle with life.
We pin our hopes on all the things that ultimately fail us, not because there is something wrong with them, but only that we expect more than they can offer.
We spend so much time trying to fix things in life to feel secure, when actually we don't need to fix them at all, we need to understand them. The moment we understand the reality of life we are free from the unhappiness that arises from the attachment to our dream states, and the consequent expectations that things will be perfect for us.
Often it seems that money, power, romance and family offer a solid base for the feelings of security we crave so much for, and whilst this may appear to be true in the conventional world, it is not true for the heart.
The heart recognises intuitively the emptiness of seeking security in a universe of phenomena that is in an endless state of change. There is nothing that can be held for even a moment, so what to do?
Everyone who has awoken to life has met this moment, from the Buddha to every disciple of Dhamma. It is called, 'the opening of the wisdom eye.' We look at our life and think there must be a better way to live than this, and there is, we just have to find it.
So now, take some time to reflect and ask yourself what you want to do with the next part of your life and remember, you may not

know what you want, but you always know what you don't want, you only have to be brave enough to listen to your heart.

Like it or not we are all connected and truth is the only thing that will serve you. Not with new age spiritual sound bites and half understood teachings, but with support from the true and loving Dhamma heart.

Transcending the needs of 'self' is the greatest gift we can bring to ourselves and all beings.

May all beings be happy.

Frustration.

Frustration is a natural movement of mind and has its base in fear. We feel that something is not going according to our own particular plan and recognising that we don't actually control anything at all, we feel vulnerable, hence the feeling that we call frustration.

The remedy of course is to 'let go' and allow everything to follow its natural path. This is difficult simply because we have been told so often by our parents and society that we need to take control, but reflect, if we cannot control this mind that we call ours, how can we control anything else?

The behaviour of other beings and even the universe itself, is often frustrating, but why?

Why are we always so concerned with situations and then the actions of fellow beings in our life?

The answer is fear, it is always fear.

Because of fear we attempt to control everyone and everything so that life will always be comfortable for us, but the Dhamma Way is to recognise our own human limitations and respond to conditions and situations as they arise, rather than reacting crying, 'it's not fair, it's not what I wanted!'

So relax a little bit.

Beings are the way they are, that is their choice.

You are the way you are, and that is your choice, and the universe is unfolding in its own particular way, moment after moment.

A peaceful and more productive life is not something outside that you can get by controlling the universe and everything in it, it begins and ends with your personal relationship to what is actually happening.

May all beings be happy.

The value of patience.

The Dhamma journey is a long one and that is why it is so important to cultivate a loving yet disciplined relationship to ourselves. We have to do what we have to do. If not we simply end up playing some sort of spiritual game, deluding ourselves and others.

There are many necessary qualities to develop in our Dhamma life, but patience and determination are important to reflect upon. The Tao te Ching tells us that; the path is straight but people love to be sidetracked. This sidetracking comes only from the mind when it seeks distraction from the often boring work of being with it as it arises and passes away, seeing our old story time and time again. However, this is the work we have to do, and as our insight or wisdom grows (Pañña) we can more and more easily identify our own personal obstacles. Impatience is definitely a big one.

A disciple wanted to leave his Master and return to the world because he felt he had not made enough progress.

"How long have you been here?" asked the Master.

"Twenty years," replied the monk.

"Oh that's not so long," continued the Master, "stay a little bit longer."

So relax, just be aware and move on. When it's time to get up, get up, when it's time to eat your meal, eat your meal and so on.......

Letting go is often a misnomer because it implies that we have to put something down, but actually it is better not to pick something up!

Just recognise that a thought is just a thought, a mood is just a mood, a feeling is just a feeling and an emotion is just an emotion. Don't allow the mind to trick you into thinking there is anything more than this.

Clouds passing through an empty sky, 'not me, not mine, not what I am'.

We must practice with humility and put down any ideas of getting somewhere or becoming something, just sit quietly and live lovingly and don't be distracted by what the mind presents in different moments.

May all beings be happy.

The infinite potential of the loving heart.

We will live happily and in peace,
simply and with integrity.
We will make love and
compassion our food,
to support and sustain us.

(Dhammapada vs 200)

There is a place of intuitive and loving recognition that manifests when the true Dhamma heart opens. A place of purity and natural integrity, far beyond the fear and greediness of 'self.' This is known as 'returning to the heart'.

Once this place of infinite Love and compassion is known, the world of politics, religion, racial and gender difference and inequality and everything it proclaims, is recognised as being empty of value.

No more delusion that can justify taking the life of a fellow being human, or any other life form that we share this planet with, no more imagination that celebrates the foolishness of a so called 'holy war', no more animal torture, cruelty and exploitation, no more eating of the flesh of others.

When the heart is open there is nothing to explain nor can be explained to those who do not understand, only a simple, powerful and beautiful life manifesting moment after moment that naturally recognises ourselves as a part of the universe, not outside manipulating and attempting to control events for our own satisfaction. No more blindly following the hostile words and actions of those seeking their prominent place in the scheme of things. 'Our troops, our religion, our land, our beliefs.' Only endless mind stuff based in fear and corruption.

When harmlessness (Ahimsa) becomes the eyes and heart that sees the world there is only the careful sharing of ourselves with Love and compassion. Never being the victim to the greed or fear of others, but recognising that everyone must meet the consequence of the mind states they empower.

When we empower fear our life becomes fearful, when we empower Love our life becomes loving. How can it be different to that?

We are all the same. Men, women, young, old, human, animal, bird, fish, tall, short, fat, thin. Those with enough, those with nothing and those with more than they can ever need. The heart intuitively recognises unity and oneness. Any speech against oneness and equality comes only from the mind of men. The heart does not discriminate because it cannot discriminate. The heart can only love.

When you have enough you can rest. When you have more than you need, you can share. In this way suffering is ended.

The foolish will laugh, but the wise know what I say.

All of Dhamma and its living manifestation to take loving care of ourselves, others and the world we are part of, is like a joke - you either get it or you don't, but it can't be explained.

May all beings be happy.

Why Pure Dhamma Retreats?
'Water boils quickly,
but it has to be on the heat for a long time'.

(Zen saying)

I have been asked to speak about the need to sit intensive Vipassana retreats in the style of Pure Dhamma, and as this is my life and the only reason to leave my small monastery to travel to other countries, I will say a few words.

In classical and traditional Dhamma teaching it is understood that there is a necessity to commit to the training fully, to see, know, understand and ultimately be free from the desire and fear based movements of mind. The insidious manifestation of 'self'.

No matter how much modern spirituality will sell the notion of instant results with very little effort, our view and more, our direct experience of students from other traditions, does not support this. If everything presented as Dhamma was understood so easily the world would be a very different place. Knowing about Dhamma is not the same thing at all as knowing Dhamma directly.

This training on retreat is simple but demanding, and far beyond rituals, guru worship, spiritual sound bites and indulgence in emotion or intellectual speculation. Although our sitting and walking practices are established in a loving supportive environment the work itself requires discipline and determination to be at peace with the mind and allow the old story of our past (kammic influences) that colours every aspect of our life, to arise in a mental atmosphere of unconditional acceptance and so be seen, known and finally released harmlessly into the universe. This is known as the Visuddhimagga, the Path of Purification.

This is the work that only we can do, but more it is the work that needs to be done to be at peace in life and everything it presents. We do not see the world as it is, we see the world as we are. How can we be free if we only cover our old story with a new one?

Therefore it is said that the true Dhamma Path is only for the brave, and more, there is no time to waste. Life is short and uncertain and if we don't awaken in this very lifetime, when will we do it?

There is the story of the hermit who left his hermitage to meet the Buddha, who was in the town collecting alms food when they met.

"Please," said the hermit, "give me a teaching."

"Friend," replied the Buddha, "this is not the time. Please come back in an hour."

The hermit was resolute in his demand. "An hour," he exclaimed, "who knows what can happen in an hour. You might be dead, or I might be dead, either way I don't receive Dhamma from you, so I ask you again, please give me a teaching."

The Buddha was so impressed by this sense of urgency that he stopped his activity and gave the hermit his teaching.

For those who consider themselves to be on the Dhamma Path as a disciple or student, this is an attitude to cultivate.

Retreats are important, but only you can know that for yourself. Excuses to stay at home or do something else may sound plausible in the moment, but in the end it is each one of us that meets the consequence of what we prioritise.

May all beings be happy.

The Way to freedom.

However difficult or awful things may seem on the surface, the Dhamma teaching is always simple; live from Love and not fear for this is where your real strength lies.

Don't empower the notion that you must control and manipulate everyone and everything in the endless and ultimately futile attempt to feel comfortable.

All of your life and every aspect of your life is about you!

Until Awakening and the freedom from self identity, it will always be like this. It's never really about somebody else, it's always about you.

But you are the architect of your life, you are designing and building your life in every moment by the mind states you empower, and then you become the recipient of the consequences of the very thing you have just created.

So take care with your life, live with Love, let the heart open and recognise that your own liberation from pain comes directly from you, and all you have to do is put down your fear.

Now, from this calm and joyful place you can respond to each moment, powerfully, elegantly and beautifully. Who can defeat you now?

This is the nature of the heart, and is waiting for you. Just let go, let go, let go.

And don't be mislead, truth has always had a hard time in the face of political, social and religious manipulation.

Base your life and all your relationships on your own direct experience and trust only your heart, your intuitive feeling. In this way your integrity will always remain secure.

May all beings be happy.

Grasping a cloud.

Until the fear within us is exhausted 'self' is always seeking to protect and present itself into every moment of life.

In the material world it manifests by endlessly becoming yet another thing to support itself, a mother, a father, a house owner, a success, a rich person, the list is endless.

In the spiritual world it is the same process, more and more holding on under the delusion of letting go. Becoming a meditator, or worse, a meditation teacher, a spiritual celebrity, a Buddhist, a Muslim, a Hindu, and any other identity it can grasp at. 'Who was I in a past life? Who will I be in my next life?'

In the end we chase something illusionary and try to make it real, but it's not, it's like trying to hold onto a cloud or smoke from incense, and so will always disappoint us.

In the end everything is fine and there is nothing to resolve and nothing left to become. Relax, exhale and let go of the fear that directs you to always look for the next thing, the next identity and step into in your life. When it is pleasant, enjoy it. When it is difficult, be patient. In the end everything resolves itself and you can be at peace. This is the whole of Dhamma.

May all beings be happy.

At peace with the uncertainty of life.

Before Awakening, what we seek is always the same as everyone else, and that is certainty in life.

We hold a belief in the superficial equation of 'if I do this I will get that.'

Sometimes it works the way we would like and other times not at all, and then everything in between. In other words, certainty does not exist in the conventional world, and so we struggle with life.

We pin our hopes on all the things that ultimately fail us, not because there is something wrong with them, but only that we expect more than they can offer.

So much of our time is spent trying to fix things in life to feel secure, when actually we don't need to fix them at all, we simply need to understand them. The moment we understand the reality of life we are free from the unhappiness that arises from the attachment to our dream states, and the consequent expectations that things will be perfect for us.

To seek happiness, comfort or any kind of certainty or security outside ourselves is to always keep ourselves as a victim, not to the world as we would like it to be, but to the mind itself.

By sustained effort and self-discipline
wise people are able to build themselves an island
that no flood can sweep away.

(Dhammapada vs 25)

May all beings be happy.

Life is not fair.

The foolish person thinks,
'these children are mine, this wealth is mine',
but we do not even own this very mind and body,
much less our children and wealth.

(Dhammapada vs 62)

Sometimes life can feel frustrating. We look around the world and see cruelty, suffering and pain and feel helpless. We don't know what to do.

No matter how much we try, even with the best intentions we cannot convince others to be kind, compassionate, honest and caring and a little voice in the head shouts, 'it's not fair.'

And that voice is right, it's not fair, but fairness is a human concept and does not exist outside the human mind. Life itself is impersonal and only an endless stream of conditions, one creating the environment for the next. An endless flow of impersonal moments continuing into infinity.

So, as disciples of Dhamma, what is our place in the moment when we feel overwhelmed by a feeling of impotence and struggle to make a fair world?

Actually the answer is unpleasantly simple.

It is the recognition that no matter how noble, how pure and how loving we feel our intentions to be, the only being we can actually take responsibility for is ourselves. We can tell stories, show pictures and argue facts but in the end Dhamma is heard or not.

We can't make others understand, we can only live a loving, caring compassionate life without intention for ourselves. We take responsibility for our own personal conduct and allow the world to go its own way. Even if we don't approve, even if we are frustrated by it, even if it's painful.

This does not mean ever, that we should simply stand by and

allow injustice and any form of cruelty and abuse to take place, but to remember that beings are the way they are, and so act accordingly. However, you are the way that you are and you need to reflect; what is my contribution to the world? More anger, more frustration, more confusion, more shouting that it's not fair, or a loving embrace of reality and then a wise response?

Dhamma is about Love, first for ourselves and then outwards to all beings, without exception. When we live from this unconditional acceptance of reality we are already free, free to accept the behaviour of the unawakened world, free to be above its cruel and unjust influence and free to respond as our heart determines.

May all beings be happy.

How can I help?

The deepest question in the world of Dhamma and also the most frustrating.

Simply and honestly we can say each of us occupy our own worlds, and so the world of the disciple is different from the world of the Master.

How can the Master show the beauty of their life when the eyes of the disciple are so often coloured by their own fears and apprehensions.

When the Buddha awakened he realised how difficult it would be to share this Dhamma with others and so he decided not to teach. However, a great compassion arose within him and he thought, 'no matter how difficult it is, my responsibility now is to share this Dhamma with whomever will listen.'

For myself, I have to walk in these footsteps, to honor the Buddha, my teacher and the Dhamma itself.

That I occasionally meet disagreement is a fact of my life, but as the truth is always impartial and I feel that I have nothing to convince others of, I truly don't mind.

In all the years I have shared this beautiful Dhamma it has never been my contention that you must believe me and do as I say. You are responsible for the quality of your world and blindly following the rules of others cannot lead to liberation.

The teaching itself is simple; live with love and be aware.

Follow this simple yet difficult Path and you will have no need to pick up more things to carry. You yourself will be happy and so share that joyful happiness with all beings.

May all beings be happy.

The Pure in Heart.

For the pure in heart there is no greed, therefore no exploitation of others.

For the pure in heart there is no fear, therefore no manipulation of others.

For the pure in heart there is only Love for all beings, therefore service to all beings.

For the pure in heart there is only compassion, therefore protection for all beings.

For the pure in heart there is integrity in all things, therefore honesty and truthfulness even in the face of untrue and unfair criticism.

For the pure in heart there is complete self responsibility, therefore an acknowledgement and acceptance of the consequence of what has gone before.

For the pure in heart there is only truth.

For the pure in heart there is only purity.

For the pure in heart there is the ultimate freedom from 'self' and the world.

When the heart is pure the world holds nothing to attract it.

This is the truest expression of Dhamma.

May all beings be happy.

The cultivation of fear.

Don't be mistaken and don't be misled by what the media presents as reality, love is everywhere.
People helping and serving the world for no reason other than they can. Caring and sharing what they have, not only in emergencies but in every aspect of their ordinary daily life.
I live in France, and if someone helps me and I thank them their usual response is 'c'est normal' - what else should I do?
Which culture is not like this?
So the problem is not lack of love, it is the cultivation of fear.
Fear appears as your friend, but truly is your greatest enemy, full of lies and misinformation. You think it will help you in your life, but it is always a tool used against you. No matter how intelligent you are, you become the victim to imagination and worse, the manipulations of those who wish to use you for their own ends.

Left by yourself, who do you want to kill?
Left by yourself, who do you hate?
Left by yourself, whose country do you want to invade?
Love is our strength and fear our weakness.

Muslims, Jews, Christians, Hindus, Buddhists, terrorists, are not born, they are made. Conditioned and programmed by others. At some point we need to ask why, and at some point we need to stop feeding the machine that encourages discrimination and mistrust. The Buddha reminds us that we should 'make ourselves an island that no flood can sweep away.' To be strong in love and trust our heart rather than what is presented as truth by those with their own agenda.
There have always been beings living amongst us who are filled with Love so that just their very presence is a gift to the world, and there have always been others, greedy and manipulative who

want to control and conquer. Our only choice is which Path do we follow, the Path of Love or the path of hatred.

Hatred is never overcome by more hatred.
Only love can overcome hatred.
This is an eternal law.

(Dhammapada vs 5)

May all beings everywhere and in all situations
be well and happy.

The loving heart of Dhamma.

Dhamma training is the Way to be free, to live with love and be aware. To find happiness for ourselves so that we can share that happiness with all beings. The greatest teachers manifest this happiness and love in their relationship with their students.

The fundamental things are the ones we have to address. Are you comfortable, are you warm, do you have enough to eat?

The Buddha himself discovered that we have to be strong and healthy to make the practice and so the basic requirements for life are the primary concern.

The real Masters are like loving fathers, hard when they need to be, but always loving. Their advice is Pure Dhamma. Take care of you, so that you can take care of others. When you have energy you will share that. When you are tired you will share that. Be something of value in the world.

There are no secrets in Dhamma. Truth is truth, love is love, wisdom is wisdom and these qualities always manifest in the simple and spontaneous acts of caring and kindness.

May all beings be happy.

The day Betty walked into the sea.

When I was a young man, so many years ago, I lived with my wife and our two sons in a small terraced house in a suburb of Douglas on the Isle of Man.

Our neighbours on both sides were very nice people but we liked our older neighbours more. They were a well educated middle aged couple with a grown family who had come to the island with their little dog Penny, to enjoy the final part of their life. Campbell was a professional person working in Douglas and Betty was a lovely roly poly woman content to be at home to cook and bake and involve herself in small charity events.

They were a happy couple!

One year Betty decided to take a small job in a local shop that sold a myriad of things including, in the October and early November months, fireworks.

Inadvertently she sold some fireworks to a young person who was, as we discovered later, under age to purchase these things.

As we don't carry any form of identification in the U.K. it's not always easy to establish a person's age and so if they say they are sixteen and look sixteen, we must accept that, or take a chance and refuse to serve them. This applies equally to young people in bars, where the legal drinking age is eighteen.

However, someone complained and the police were called. Betty was charged and was required to appear before the Deemster (the judge on the Isle of Man).

The charge was not particularly serious and the maximum penalty would be a small fine or a simple warning to take greater care in future.

When we heard about this we merely shrugged our shoulder and said, "poor Betty, she'll get over it."

But Betty didn't get over it and this disgrace as she saw it, weighed heavily upon her mind.

One morning in secret she boarded the boat to England. After the four hour sea journey to Heysham, she took the train just a few minutes further down the coast, and on a cold November morning, stood on the beach at the waters edge, took off all her clothes and walked into the sea. She drowned.

Suffering is a word in common use in many forms of spiritual understanding, and although it may be entertaining to compare one persons apparent suffering to another, it is always fruitless.

In Dhamma terms the word suffering is defined as 'that which is difficult to bear' and so it will always be unique and personal to the individual.

What is considered suffering for one person may be nothing at all for another. Naturally because of this we must assess each situation individually and compassionately and offer our help and support without indulging the person too much.

We can only be of service to those carrying this enormous weight by leaving them space to lift themselves up and so be free from this burden which for them, is so 'difficult to bear.'

The beauty of our loving Dhamma is to serve the world with universal kindness. This, in the end becomes our greatest gift.

May all beings be happy.

All is One.

Don't kill baby humans.
Don't kill baby cows.
Don't kill baby sheep.
Don't kill baby goats.
Don't kill baby chicks.
Don't kill baby pigs.
Don't kill their parents either.
And don't pay someone to do it for you.
Life is simple if we remember that it is precious for all beings, and so I say;

'May all beings be happy and secure, may their hearts be wholesome.
Whatever living beings there may be, feeble or strong, tall, stout or medium, long, short or small, seen or unseen, those living far or near, those who are born and those who are to be born, may all beings, without exception, be happy minded.'
This is the teaching of Love. The teaching of Oneness. The teaching of Freedom.

May all beings be happy.

True Awakening.

Don't think that Awakening is easy – it's not.
It's simple, but never easy because Awakening is always an unlearning process, to let go and let go and let go until there is nothing more to let go of.
This is the Path to complete liberation from our unhappiness, but who is really prepared to do this? To become a beautiful nobody.
The heart seeks nothing, whilst the head wants everything.
The heart says 'leave me alone in my beauty' whilst the head shouts 'I know, I have ideas, I have understood everything!'
We must realise that 'Master' exists only in the mind of the disciple, it does not exist in the mind of the Master.
For him or her there is no more attachment or identification as being someone or something existing in time and space, only the transcendent flowingness with life.
The power of this now radiant invisibility can be felt in every moment and in every situation. This is the gift to the world.
No more religious views and opinions, only the wisdom of direct immersion into truth. Beyond words, beyond gestures, beyond rites and rituals.
So our Path is clear. To 'get out of our own way', until all that is left is the heart. Without this direct realisation of truth, you cannot know the reality and elegant beauty of simply being.
No more fear, only Love.
No more compromise, only compassion.
No more views and opinions, only wisdom.
Awakening is never easy, but it is the greatest thing in the universe.
Work hard to 'get out of your own way'.

May all beings be happy.

Going beyond 'self'.

Just because you're angry doesn't mean you're right.
Just because you believe something doesn't mean it's true.
Just because you're intelligent doesn't mean you're wise.
Just because you're human doesn't mean you're superior.
Humility is the key to liberation, and Love is the key to humility. To know yourself as part of the whole and not outside judging or exploiting is the Way to peace and peace will be the gift in your life that you will spontaneously share with others.

May all beings be happy.

Naked in Dhamma.

All the barriers you erect to protect yourself from pain in life must ultimately be dissolved and so allow you to experience the world as it is and no longer simply as your fear tells you it is.

Those personal, ego designed spectacles that colour everything you see must be discarded so the heart can fully understand the foolishness we fill our life with.

Without Love, we are lost, and as much as we rationalise and then display our fear, it is forever a trap to keep us small.

Letting go is the Way of Dhamma, and Love, compassion and generosity towards all beings is the manifestation of our open caring heart.

When the emptiness of self identity is truly understood, life is finally seen as the Dhamma blessing it always has been.

May all beings be happy.

Dukkha, Dukkha, Dukkha.
(Unsatisfactoryness)

The Buddha has said that there are three kinds of Dukkha or 'unsatisfactoryness' that we meet as living beings.

The first is Dukkha Dukkha, or the unsatisfactoryness connected to the physical body. Traditionally we speak about old age, sickness and death and these are qualities that will be known to all beings taking birth.
To meet these conditions means that we are alive and even if they are uncomfortable, without life we could not experience them. Happily their nature is to be impermanent and so whatever arises will pass in one way or another.
A loving patience is a true gift we can bring to our own life.

The second manifestation of Dukkha is called Viparinama Dukkha, the unsatisfactoryness connected to the experience of everything in a constant process of change. Without wisdom it is easy to fall into the trap of seeking security in the things that are by their very nature, moving away from us, trying to hold things that have already passed even by the time we have reached out our hand.
This flow of all phenomena is called Anicca and is a truth that needs a thorough investigation if we wish to live peacefully in a universe that we don't control.

The third manifestation of Dukkha is called Sankhara Dukkha, and to express it without elaboration, means the unsatisfactoryness we experience in life by simply not being awakened.
Upon Awakening everything is seen, known and understood according to its nature. There is no more grasping and no more rejecting and so a life and a way to be, in perfect harmony.

When we bump into the struggles of life, this is what we meet, and so the teachings of liberation are always directly in front of us. We only have to remind ourselves not to be deluded by the appearance of things.

May all beings be happy

Perfect practice.

The Pure Dhamma tradition of Love and Awareness does not belong to the world of ambition and achievement, and so it is never a good idea to set yourself targets and goals in the practice, but to simply sit everyday without aim or expectation.

In this way you will open the doors to all possibilities without looking for special signs and checking the spiritual scoreboard to see how far you have come since the last time you looked.

Insight, and full Awakening itself, only happens when 'you' are not there. So the practice is to sit without waiting to get something, but to allow the intuitive understanding to arise naturally that what we call 'self' (I, me, mine and my) are simple movements of mind. Useful in the mundane world when claiming your seat on a flight, or your turn in a queue, but not much more than that!

Where there is 'self', there is suffering and so the more you intuitively see through the delusion of a permanent and enduring 'self', the happier, more loving and less stressful your life will be. You will function fully in the world, but be at peace with the results of your endeavours.

It is said that Pure Dhamma practice is like walking out on a long journey in the mist or fog, and slowly, slowly without realising it you become soaking wet.

Understanding is like this, perhaps not realising how far you have come until it reveals itself in a new and unexpected moment of life.

This is the way to give ourselves to perfect practice. To lose ourselves in an unambitious approach to Dhammic cultivation by simply doing what needs to be done rather than trying to become more spiritual.

May all beings be happy.

Just stop talking.

Only in the silence will you hear your heart.
Only in the silence will you see that your desires are endless.
Only in the silence will you see that fear is not your friend.
Only in the silence will you see that Love is always the solution.
Only in the silence will you see that what we call 'you' is only an endless process of change.
Only in the silence will you see that words are always inadequate, and your presence and behaviour is what the world feels.
Only in the silence will you see the interconnection between all beings and that pain is pain, fear is fear and suffering is suffering.
Only in the silence will you see that your ideas and opinions are only more chatter from the mind.
Only in the silence will you see the emptiness of life, and that what we make important is only important because we make it so.
Only in the silence will you see the truth that is beyond the fears and fantasies of mind, that you are already free, you always were free and you always will be free.
Only in the silence will you meet the truth.

May all beings fall silent, if only for a moment.
May all beings be happy.

Serving the world without conditions.

The difficult truth to accept for all serious practitioners of Dhamma is that in every moment we are actually helpless in the emotional and spiritual lives of others no matter who they are. We can support, encourage, insist, beg, manipulate, but in the end how others live and what they empower comes only from them.

I sit in front of disciples and students and say simply, 'live with love and be aware,' but in every instance we all hear something different according to our own level of understanding.

The reality is that only when we truly know ourselves will we know others, and no matter how persuasive our arguments may be people will not stop eating meat or dairy products, they will not stop smoking or drinking alcohol, they will not be kinder or more loving until they themselves see the need to change something in their life.

I offer Dhamma to all beings and make no demands that others follow my Way.

I do not kill or encourage others to kill.

I do not steal or encourage others to steal.

I do not abuse or manipulate fellow beings or encourage others to abuse or manipulate fellow beings.

I do not use my speech in cruel or harmful ways or encourage others to use their speech in cruel or harmful ways.

I do not take drugs to alter the consciousness or encourage others to take drugs to alter their consciousness.

I live as lovingly and purely as I can, and take responsibility for myself and my conduct. This is the Way of Dhamma.

May all beings be happy.

Finding the true Master

When you are deliberately looking for a Master, it is not surprising that suddenly someone will present themselves as exactly what you want.

They will shine in front of you, and blind you with their words and enlightened behaviour, until you fall in love with them and become a true follower.

Slowly then comes the beginning of your mental athletics and endless compromising to ensure this person always fits your fantasies of what a Master should be.

Perhaps they will inadvertently reveal their deep seated hidden desires and aversions, but upon questioning, will always be able to present a satisfactory Dhammic explanation of them, and you in your trust and naivety, will seek a truth in their words and what is presented in front of you, but sooner or later the heart speaks and this will be the first step on your own true Path.

No one can save you. No one can free you from your past. No one can purify your heart, only you can do that. And this is the truth of liberation.

We are our own saviours. The Master points the Way but asks for nothing in return.

Reflect: if the Master is a fully realised being, what could they possibly want from you?

In the end everything is teaching us, but often it takes time to understand the lesson.

Take care with who you sit in front of.

May all beings be happy.

The Path of Love.

Violence does not belong to the heart and so cannot be a part of our loving Way of Dhamma.

Violence belongs to the mind, the mind of 'self', the mind of fear, the mind of division, the mind of hatred.

When the heart is open all beings are intuitively recognised as having equal value, no above or below, no in front or behind, no greater or lesser, only universal equality, and so to harmonise with the world of the heart is to find perfect peace in life. Naturally arising then is the pure intention to serve, to protect, to encourage, to love. These are the qualities of the compassionate caring heart. However, the world is filled with unawakened beings, with each person seeking the same sense of security and stability in life, but always looking in the wrong place. Because of this need to feel comfortable and secure, devices that promise such things become a commodity that can be traded - now we enter the world of politics, social manipulation and religious beliefs. These are all mind born entities and whereas the heart simply accepts and responds with kindness, this mind exploits either grossly or subtly, the perceived weakness of others.

This is why the world is as we see it. It's not nature and it's not inevitable but it is the reality of the moment, and that, no matter how painful it can be, is what we must accept, simply because it is the reality. Reality is always unrelenting and so arising from that, if we have clear eyes, we can see our place in this often unkind and confused way of being.

We must reflect honestly, 'what is it that I contribute to this world, more fear based ideologies or a loving embrace of all beings?'

Anything that brings us to this fearless state of Love can be considered a gift in our life. The moment we intuitively understand that Love is always the answer, we will share the most beautiful part of ourselves with all beings without reservation or resistance.

Those who argue for wars and support any kind of violent behaviour towards others illuminate the way of delusion and so become the gifts in our life. Because of this lighting of darkness, we can see a more beautiful way to live and so firmly establish ourselves on the Path of Love.

May all beings be happy.

The essence of practice.

The secret of practice is to actually just do it and not allow the mind to trick you into giving up. Consistency of effort is how to build up the conviction that our practice of Love and Awareness is the principle movement in life that has true value.

To be consistent and not feel disappointment with how you perceive your practice is progressing, you need to stop demanding that you are suddenly a perfect being, never making mistakes or having uncomfortable thoughts, but being at peace with the mind as it arises and passes away, and to live with Love and Awareness as best you can in each moment.

Don't make excuses to justify poor behaviour but see each incident as an opportunity to develop the intuitive understanding of the value of what you do.

Of course, it's not always easy.

When the first days of excitement for this new meditation venture have passed we may develop a very different relationship to our practice. However, this is when the real value of training comes to the forefront - to just do it no matter what the voices in your head say!

Sometimes it's boring, sometimes tiring, sometimes just not interesting enough, but this is just the Mara mind telling you to do something that is superficially more gratifying but will always keep you tied to the world, like a calf to its mother.

The Dhamma response then, is simple, don't listen and do what you're supposed to do in both the sitting practice and relating to the world to the best of your ability.

This is not a race or a contest, and the only pressure you might feel, is coming from you. Pure Dhamma is a gentle, loving Way. A Way to allow the old habits of mind to arise, to see them, know them and release their power harmlessly into the universe. It is called 'the Way of letting go.'

Often it is only our own high expectations of ourselves that take us to a sense of failure, but you must remember, if Dhamma was so easy, everyone would be awakened!
So relax a little bit and take one moment at a time. Don't put yourself under pressure to be the perfect being you have imagined yourself to be and remember that Love begins with ourselves.
Our Dhamma journey is long and it needs a loving patience and a determined attitude to see it through to the end.

May all beings be happy.

The perfection in Pure Dhamma practice.

Here we just sit quietly opening our heart so that the old story we carry, the old habit of grasping at who and what we are, can be seen, accepted and finally released harmlessly into the universe. Now we are no longer a victim to those old voices and our conditioning and so, whatever we meet in the mind, whatever thought, mood, feeling, or emotion, whatever idea, mental projection into the future or memory of past deeds, is absolutely perfect in this moment.

We don't have to get rid of anything, or create something different, something spiritual to experience.

In this place, life is just life in the most beautiful way. The complaining mind falls quiet and things are seen to be only what they are, not good or bad, right or wrong, but events happening in time and space. We can interact or not. We can choose our response to each moment knowing that whatever we do will resonate with the pure hearted beings or not.

Do not think that you are not seen by the pure in heart. You are known by the thoughts you empower, Love or fear, compassion or greed, generosity or selfishness.

The moment we free ourselves from the narrow limitations of the mind that is always chasing the next moment of happiness, we are free, and in that freedom we will see that whatever this old voice says, everything is perfect.

> May all beings live in peace,
> may all beings be happy.

No - Self.

When people confidently say that there is no 'self' they are expressing a profound misunderstanding of the Buddha's teaching of Anatta.

In truth, such a statement should never be used.

There is 'self', but the lifespan of this 'self' lasts only a moment and is then superseded by the next brief moment of 'self'. A new 'self', conditioned by the old one in an endless cycle of what we call life.

This process of 'self' arising and passing away happens countless times a moment and is completely impersonal, although always conditioned by karmic forces.

At the same time there is also a conventional reality of 'self' arriving in the world, something that appears to be real and substantial, something that endures and is a valid and true identity. When this 'self' arises, a whole history arises, manifesting as 'I was in the past, I am now, I will be in the future.'

This false understanding of 'self' does not recognise the reality of the moment to moment flow of 'beingness' and foolishly presents itself in ego based language as 'I, me, mine.'

Understanding the truth of Anatta is fundamental to our spiritual Awakening and to help explain it more simply, perhaps the analogy of the river is useful.

When we use the word river we all know what is meant, a body of water, something fixed in time and space and easy to identify.

However, river of course, is only a concept, and the reality is that every part of this concept is in an endless state of change. The water flows, it evaporates and is refilled by rain and small streams, animals and fish live in the water and swim and interact leaving their own imprint, insects on the surface of the water play their part and finally there is the natural erosion of the banks due to time and the seasons.

Now we can see that the river is not one fixed thing but actually it is an endless process of change.

'Self' is like this.

This moment of 'self' conditions the next and the next and so on and so on.

The word 'beingness' is used to express the understanding of this impersonal process and the harmonious acceptance of it.

Once the habitual and delusive attachment to a self identity with all its fears and desires falls away, there is peace. No more grasping and no more rejecting, only a natural response to life with Love, compassion and wisdom.

When the delusion of a fixed 'self identity' is transcended it cannot re-establish itself which is why Awakening is always understood as letting go completely, rather that acquiring a new identity or ability.

As the Buddha said, 'even if I use the word 'self' I am never deluded by it.'

'Self' is real - just not in the way you think it is.

May all beings be happy.

The purity of Love.

In the whole history of life, fear, hatred and anger are the three conditions of mind that have never brought a worthy solution to any difficulty.
If this is all you have to offer you are never helping the situation.

With fear, you cannot see.
With hatred you cannot hear.
With anger you cannot be compassionate.

As always, listen to your heart, not those who wish to manipulate you for their own ends. For every bullet fired, for every bomb exploded, for every life taken, someone is making a profit.
Love is the answer, because Love can never be defeated.
It is only Love that will save you and all beings from the suffering of life.
If you truly understood the power of Love, fear would have no place in your heart.

May all beings be happy.

Such is life.

Balancing the things we want against the things we don't want is the game of life. Trying so desperately to fill our time with wonderful things such as romance, love, family, money, comfort, security always at the expense of the things that we don't want, old age, illness, pain, discomfort and insecurity.

With wisdom we will see and know for ourselves, that it is all empty and life however it manifests, is neither for you nor against you and in fact, it's just life. With this simple realisation we can play this game with a joyful heart and appreciate the pleasant things when we have them, before they slip from our grasp, and be with the more difficult things knowing that with wise understanding, we are always able to let them go.

When the heart is truly open we neither grasp nor reject but simply accept the reality of the moment as it manifests and then respond with whatever action is necessary.

This is how our ordinary life manifests the Four Noble Truths of the Buddha, and how we can use it as our own Path to liberation.

May all beings be happy.

Drugs and Dhamma.

It is true that in many cultures the use of hallucinogenics is accepted as part of a spiritual path, but it is not so in orthodox Buddhist or Dhamma teachings. The function of our meditation practice is to clear and purify the mind, so that reality can be experienced as it is, rather than as an emotional reaction to internal or external events or a drug induced fantasy.

This highest practice therefore is 'just to sit' and be with things 'as they are'.

Naturally this kind of practice is not always exciting or even interesting and so demands real commitment. In the end it is exactly what the Buddha had to do. He had been a prince and renounced that life of comfort and convenience because, even though he had everything, it was never enough so he let go of his confidence in the world to bring complete satisfaction and became a wandering ascetic.

But even then nothing really changed. He could never give enough away. There was always one less grain of rice he could eat, one more comfort he could give up, one more humiliating practice he could attempt. This is the way of life when we simply follow the mind without looking into its real nature, and so, in the end he realised that nothing worked. Trying to achieve enlightenment by following the mind was like trying to walk to the horizon, no matter how fast he appeared to move it always stayed the same distance away.

And so he stopped!

He stopped grasping at new situations, new spiritual experiences, he stopped destroying himself for something that was only an imagination, and he stayed still. Now for the first time he saw the mind with its endless desires and aversions, none of which took him to peace but only to more confusion and doubt.

When the mind is clear the truth is always right in front of us and so as disciples of Dhamma we stop looking for distractions and diversions and open ourselves to the infinite peace of the spacious mind. No longer grasping, no longer rejecting but letting go of the movements of mind that do not take us to peace.

May all beings be happy.

The warmth of Dhamma.

When true Dhamma understanding takes root in our heart it illuminates everything. It is like the sun rising in the morning, slowly but beautifully spreading it's golden light into even the darkest corners.

Now we can see clearly and so will bring something of value into each situation we find ourselves in.

The intuitive knowing that our old habits of blaming our unhappiness on others is empty spontaneously changes our relationship with the world, and so all beings.

Love does not rely on chanting or ceremony but only on the compassionate recognition that 'all is one' and that everyone has 'our face,' and then how that manifests into life.

We do not seek our happiness in others but rather live to share our joy with the world.

Nothing is greater than Love, and true Love comes only from a Pure Dhamma understanding of our real self, and life.

May all beings be happy.

We are here.

One practice worthy of our greatest effort is that of gratitude.
Although we sometimes feel that life can be hard and unrelenting it is still a fact that everything that we have ever met in our life since the first moment of birth has brought us to this place now, for better or for worse.
It is gratitude that allows us to value our story and to appreciate the Dhamma journey that we are taking.
The basis of gratitude then is acceptance. To recognise that the reality of the moment as we meet it, is only the consequence of the mind states we have empowered. It is impersonal in one sense and deeply personal in another.
The world we experience is the one that we create for ourselves moment after moment and this world is always unique and personal to us. No one can enter this personal world as we cannot enter the world of another and so the pain and difficulties that we meet belongs only to ourselves as does our sense of appreciation and gratitude.
To understand the subtlety of the mind we must stop our usual daily activity and surrender. This stopping we call meditation and in our tradition of Pure Dhamma it is known as Vipassana, the Way to see things as they really are.
By sitting silently and letting go of all expectation we meet the mind. Our mind. The mind we have cultivated through all these years. This is the most important and necessary practice for without it we will always attempt to justify and rationalise our habit of simply following the mind like a monkey jumping from branch to branch.
It may feel good in the moment, but its direction is always circular, leading us back to the same, old and familiar place.
We judge our life on our old story filled with its habits of accepting and rejecting and so what we consider to be hard or difficult is

only valued on this comparison.
Reflect, what you consider to be uncomfortable or frustrating may not mean anything to anyone else.
So the teaching is always the same.
Relax, be patient and just do what you're supposed to do.
One day you will look back on the difficult moments of your life and see the Dhamma value of them.
This is the correct way to train.

May all beings be happy.

A skillful life.
Our practice is not only about sitting in meditation, it is about all the times we are not sitting in meditation.

To establish our daily life on the habit of meditation is a wonderful foundation for developing our Dhamma heart, but if we leave our peace and joy on our cushion it has very little value.

Always I speak about Dhamma as a living practice and not simply an escape from the world for half an hour a day and the Buddha reminds us of this when he tells us that this beautiful Way of Love and Awareness can be practiced in the four postures of sitting, standing, walking and lying down. This means that there is never an obstacle to our Path except the one the mind creates with its excuses and laziness.

However, we do need to be aware of our old habits and the quiet power of them as in reality, changing our life is mostly about remembering to be different - different from simply following the mind wherever it leads us and then so often pointing the finger of blame at someone else for what we do and how we feel.

The value of the cultivation of Love cannot be over estimated and I emphasise its practice at all times. To wish all other beings without any exceptions happiness and peace in their life, even if we don't like them or approve of their actions. To reflect upon our life and how much we contribute to the pain and suffering in the world through our speech and actions, and then what we can do to refine our behaviour.

Entering into a vegetarian or better, a vegan lifestyle is good for you, the animal kingdom and the planet we are all part of. Burgers might be a convenient food choice, but the life of an animal has been taken simply for that convenience.

Love and compassion are shown in many different ways, not always by something dramatic in our life, but more often the simple recognition that all beings have the capacity to suffer. Once we understand the pain of suffering for ourselves the heart cannot deliberately inflict that same pain onto any other being, whether it is by our own hand or someone paid to do it on our behalf.

Before Awakening our life is always about ourselves. It is our first thought in the morning and our last thought at night, and always phrased in the silent question, 'how can I be happy?'

However, as the heart opens that very thought naturally becomes less intense as we realise that the true feelings of Love, compassion and interconnectedness with the universe are part of is where true happiness really lives.

All beings fear pain and death.
Remembering that we are one of them,
we will neither hurt nor kill.

(Dhammapada vs 129)

May all beings be happy

Stop killing things!
(The need for Ahimsa)

It seems that there are so many men and women who have a voracious thirst for taking life, from each other in the case of war and religious violence, to weekend hunters chasing down animals for sport. Not forgetting of course the highly organised meat and dairy farming industry, big game hunting in exotic countries and pesticides and other poisons poured onto the earth. Death fills each moment of every day.

Why is it so? Are we so insecure as humans that we have to continually show our superiority by destroying each other and the planet we are part of?

When ancient mankind saw a large animal they would kill it to eat its flesh and so take its power, but now there is no reason at all for anyone to kill any other being for food. The earth is rich in all the proteins, vitamins and health giving and supportive nutrients we can ever need, and all we have to do is reflect a little bit and live a much more loving and caring life.

For the dairy industry with its smiling cow posters we see day old calves dragged away from their mothers so humans can have the milk made specifically for these new born babies, who are naturally then sold, killed and eaten some short time later.

If you are a parent now, reflect on this. Our children are precious to us, why would it be different for other species?

The question of how to make the best bacon sandwich continues with the answer, first kill a pig! That is a high price to ask for a simple snack.

In every moment each one of us has the potential to be beautiful and serve the world by bringing something of value to the planet we are all part of, or continue in our blindness and ignorance to be a part of the continuation of suffering for ourselves and other beings.

Ahimsa (harmlessness) is highly praised as the greatest Dhamma attribute and development by every great Master and it's actually very easy - just stop killing things.

If you do not work in a slaughter house or are in someway connected to this brutal industry, stop paying others to do this dreadful work for you.

And even if we say that the Buddha said it was acceptable to eat the flesh of murdered animals provided three conditions were met, that was in a place and time very, very different from our own now, so the question is always, not what do you think the Buddha said or meant but more, what do you think, because no matter how much you can point a finger and say, 'he said it's alright,' you are still the customer and the protagonist in this action. Without the customer there will be no slaughtered animal lying in pieces on the floor.

You are responsible for you both physically and mentally and you must meet the consequence of the mind states you empower.

Love and compassion will always bring a good result to the environment you are part of, whilst hatred or perhaps even worse, a lack of empathy for other beings brings an uncomfortable result sooner or later.

If you truly want to know what pain feels like for an animal, go to your home, take a hammer, put your thumb on the table and hit it. There, now you know and if there is love in your heart you would not wish even this small and localized pain onto another being.

We are human beings, supposedly the highest life form on the planet, how then can we justify the cruel and unjust treatment of other living beings simply for our own convenience? These are my thoughts today.

May all beings without exception be happy.

The truth of happiness.
Happiness is happiness, but happiness is suffering.

At one time on retreat a woman came to my room and spoke to me;
"You're always talking about happiness," she said," but I don't want to be happy, I want to be peaceful."
"And if you were peaceful," I replied, "what then?"
"Oh, then I'd be happy," she finished.

There is a common assumption that when we speak to each other we understand completely what is being said by the choice of the words used, but this is never the case.

Although we may use what appears to be a common language, in reality the nuance of each word will be unique to each one of us, based on our own personal relationship with life.

So, for example, when I say 'dog' perhaps you hear, 'warm, cuddly, friendly little animal, man's best friend and a joy to have around', or perhaps you hear, 'dangerous and potentially savage animal that should never be allowed into a house'.

The word is the same but the understanding is different and unique.

It is the same with Dhamma language. Whatever you think I'm saying, I am only ever speaking about Love, and encouraging you to find the place of complete acceptance in your heart, for all beings.

Happiness is a powerful word and one that we all know well and use often, but how we understand happiness in different moments will always be based upon our own personal interpretation.

Happiness itself is an impermanent moment of mind and so to base a life around this feeling can only lead to disappointment and frustration.

Actually, happiness is an umbrella word. It denotes any kind of pleasant feeling, and so because pleasant feelings are in fact, pleasant, we chase after them, grasp them and attempt to hold on to them.

This of course is not the Way of Dhamma.

The word happiness is only a superficial and convenient way to speak and the goal of true Dhamma training is to transcend the simple notion of happiness and unhappiness and be at peace with the mind as it manifests moment after moment. This Way of being is in fact, higher than happiness.

So, when the mind stops grasping at different moments there is the complete feeling of being at peace with things as they are.

May all beings be happy.

Why say, 'May all beings be happy?'

When we say, may all beings be happy, we are expressing our interconnected wish that all beings, however they may manifest in the universe, are free from harm, free from fear and experience a security and safety in life.

It is a shortcut, from the Buddhist tradition and comes from the Metta Sutta. Happiness is an umbrella word to mean any feeling that is not based in fear and so, taken from our own direct experience of life and the difficulties and frustrations it may present we express from our own heart to theirs, this wish without conditions.

May all beings be happy and secure, may their hearts be wholesome.

Whatever living beings there may be, feeble or strong, tall, stout or medium, long, short or small, seen or unseen, those living far or near, those who are born and those who are to be born, may all beings, without exception, be happy minded.

May all beings be happy.

Also by Michael Kewley

1994: Higher than Happiness (Revised edition: 2014)
   Mehr als nur glücklich sein (German version)

1996: Vipassana, the way to an awakened life (Revised edition: 2013)
   Vipassana, der Weg in ein erwachtes Leben (German version)

1999: Not This (Revised edition: 2013)

1999: Life Changing Magic (Revised edition: 2009)

2006: Walking the Path (Second Edition: 2007)

2007: The Other Shore

2009: Life is not Personal
   Nimm das Leben nicht persönlich (German version)

2007: The Reality of Kamma

2011: Buttons in the Dana Box
   Knöpfe in der Dana Box (German version)

2011: The Dhammapada

2015: Loving Awareness

2017: A journey to Awakening (autobiography)

About the author

Michael Kewley is the former Buddhist monk Paññadipa, who is now an internationally acclaimed Master of Dhamma, presenting courses and meditation retreats throughout the world. For many years he was the guiding teacher at the International Meditation Centre, Budh Gaya, India and is the founder of the Pure Dhamma tradition of spiritual Awakening.

A disciple of the late Sayadaw Rewata Dhamma, he teaches solely on the instruction of his own Master; to share the Dhamma, in the spirit of the Buddha, so that all beings might benefit. On 26th May 2002, during a special ceremony at the Dhamma Talaka Temple in England, he was awarded the title of Dhammachariya.

A full biography of Michael Kewley, including videos and Dhamma talk extracts, can be found at:

www.puredhamma.org

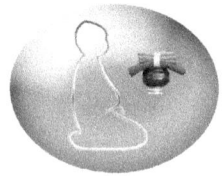

The face of Dhamma

www.ingramcontent.com/pod-product-compliance
Lightning Source LLC
LaVergne TN
LVHW051129080426
835510LV00018B/2314